GREAT HOLLYWOOD
Wit

ALSO BY GENE SHALIT

☆

Laughing Matters:
A Celebration of American Humor

*Compiled and
Edited by*

★

GENE SHALIT

GREAT HOLLYWOOD
Wit

A Glorious Cavalcade
of Hollywood Wisecracks,
Zingers, Japes,
Quips, Slings, Jests,
Snappers &
Sass from the Stars

ST. MARTIN'S PRESS
New York

BOOK DESIGN BY AMANDA DEWEY

Library of Congress Cataloging-in-Publication Data

Great Hollywood wit : a glorious cavalcade of Hollywood wisecracks, zingers, japes, quips, slings, jests, snappers & sass from the stars / [compiled by] Gene Shalit.—1st ed.
      p. cm.
   Includes bibliographical references (page 203).
   ISBN 0-312-28272-9
   1. Motion pictures—Quotations, maxims, etc.
   2. Motion picture actors and actresses—United States—Quotations. I. Shalit, Gene, 1936–

PN1994.9. G73 2002
791.43—dc21   2002068122

ISBN 0-312-28272-9

First Edition: November 2002

10   9   8   7   6   5   4   3   2   1

FOR MANY DAYS OF LOVE AND LAUGHTER.

Peter, Willa, Emily, Amanda, Nevin, Andrew

Contents

Every age has its pleasures, its style
of wit, and its own ways.
—NICOLAS BOILEAU–DESPRÉAUX

We've Got to Start Someplace, Why Not Here?

The richest harvest of humor is reaped in fields of entertainment. What other area of human endeavor can match it for merriment? Even if you search all the lib-long day, you'll never find volumes like these:

101 Funniest Accountants: The Sequel
The Wit and Wisdom of Cleaners & Dyers
A Treasury of Memorable Remarks by Kosher Butchers

Show business is a mine of humor. Example: "Hey, that joke is mine!"

A principle subdivision of show business is Hollywood, which reigns as the primary source of fertilized gossip, lies, misattributed anecdotes, set-ups, put-downs, wisecracks, apocrypha, true wit, and misanthropic mischief.

Hollywood is renowned for its backstabbing, front stabbing, revenge, envy, promises, rogues, deceit, scoundrels, geniuses, semigeniuses, quasigeniuses, former geniuses, deciduous loyalty, flagrant dreams, brains, bodies, breasts, butts, buffoons, mountebanks, intellectuals, and many intelligent good-hearted souls.

When a story or wisecrack travels from one person to another (what Sam Goldwyn called "mouth to mouth"), it may be embellished, swollen, condensed, distorted, or dehumorized—but the best endure, ever fresh, ever funny. Hence, hance, honce, this book. Who knows who *really* said this stuff first? Some japes were composed by underlings and credited to their overlings. Did Sam Goldwyn himself exclaim, "Include me out"? Or did his press agent make it up for the boss to curry favor? And did Goldwyn even *like* curried favor?

Occasional remarks were so telling that people have been telling them for years, ascribing them to whoever's handy. Many quotes are impossible to trace to their original source. Some are surely apocryphal. The truth is, some may never have been said at all, so I don't know how they got into this book.

Oscar Levant got it right when he said (and it really was Oscar who said it), "It doesn't matter who says it first; it's who gets credit for it last that counts."

So the point is not whether or not Lincoln himself wrote the Gettysburg Address. What counts is that the world will surely note and long remember what we quote here. Let us all here and now dedicate, consecrate, and forever heed the words of the late Wm. Shakespeare:

Laugh yourselves into stitches.
> —*Twelfth Night* (You can look it up. I did.)

About the Title

GREAT HOLLYWOOD *Wit*

"Analyzing wit is like dissecting a frog," said the French writer André Maurois. "When you take it apart you find out what it's made of, but the subject is killed in the process."

I have no idea what wit is.

OSCAR LEVANT

☆

Wit has truth in it; wisecracking is simply calisthenics with words.　　**DOROTHY PARKER**

☆

"Wit and caustic humor are rarely polite," Leo Rosten said. "It is always impudent, irreverent, corrosive, and somewhat arrogant."

☆

That leads to Hollywood's maxim: "If you can't say something nasty about someone, don't say anything at all."

☆

For the purposes of this gathering, *wit* has been stretched to its elastic limits. These pages are rampant with acidic, biting, sarcastic, astringent, ribald, flippant, insolent, scornful, amusing, poisonous insults, quips, repartee, one-liners, snipes, retorts, slings, bon mots, put-downs, comebacks, boasts, malapropisms, and tongue-tangled howlers—all of them funny, or revealing, or alarming.

GREAT **HOLLYWOOD** *Wit*

Hollywood is used here as a generic term for anyone, or anything, or any place connected, however tenuously, to motion pictures, from Westwood to Eastwood, from Oscars to Mayer.

GREAT HOLLYWOOD *Wit*

That I leave to you.

GREAT HOLLYWOOD
Wit

Shooting Stars
(mostly at each other)

Every actor has a natural animosity toward every
other actor, present or absent, living or dead.
LOUISE BROOKS, actress

That Heston is a nice guy, but what a hamola.

ALDO RAY, actor

☆

Shirley MacLaine—who does she think she isn't?

YVES MONTAND, French actor,
reflecting on MacLaine's past lives

☆

Get John out of the saddle and you've got trouble.

JOAN CRAWFORD, actress,
describing John Wayne, actor

☆

I'm no actor, and I have sixty-four pictures to prove it.

VICTOR MATURE, actor

☆

Alec Baldwin is this big new alleged sex symbol. But he has eyes like a weasel. He makes Clint Eastwood look like a flirt.

SANDY DENNIS, actress

☆

She ought to know about closeups. Jesus, she was around when they invented them! The bitch has been around forever!

BETTE DAVIS, when told Lillian Gish looked wonderful in a close-up in *The Whales of August*

☆

Your idea of fidelity is not having more than one man in bed at the same time.

DIRK BOGARDE, actor, to Julie Christie, actress, in *Darling* (1965)

☆

My jokes are one of the reasons Liz Taylor went on a diet. When I took her to SeaWorld and Shamu the Whale jumped out of the water, she asked if it came with vegetables.

JOAN RIVERS, actress, comedienne on Elizabeth Taylor, actress

☆

There is not enough money in Hollywood to lure me into making another picture with Joan Crawford. And I like money.

STERLING HAYDEN, actor,
of Joan Crawford, actress

☆

That obstinate, suspicious, egocentric, maddening, and lovable genius of a problem child.

MARY PICKFORD describing Charlie Chaplin.

☆

I've always hated that damn James Bond. I'd like to kill him.

SEAN CONNERY, actor

☆

Heston's the only man who could drop out of a cubic moon, he's so square. The trouble with him is he doesn't think he's just a hired actor, like the rest of us. He thinks he's the entire production. He used to sit there in the mornings and clock us with a stopwatch.

RICHARD HARRIS, Heston's
costar in *Major Dundee* (1965)

☆

Clark Gable's an idiot. You know why he's an actor? It's the only thing he's smart enough to do.

JOHN WAYNE, actor

☆

I didn't know Judy Garland well, but after watching her in action I didn't want to know her well.

JOAN CRAWFORD, actress

☆

He's the sort of guy if you say, "Hiya, Clark, how are ya?" he's stuck for an answer.

AVA GARDNER, actress, describing ex-lover
Clark Gable, actor

☆

[Katharine Hepburn] is a legend, but once you get beyond that, she's just a cranky old broad . . .

NICK NOLTE after they starred in
the failure *Grace Quigley* (1984)

☆

I'm not nearly as cranky as I should have been with him. . . . He was getting drunk in every gutter in town.

KATHARINE HEPBURN, actress,
responding to Nolte, actor

☆

Arnold Schwarzenegger is a farce. In a more sophisticated culture, he would have remained a body cultist. In America, he is not only a movie star, he has political power. The son of a Nazi, yet what the father did should be separate from what the son does. But this Schwarzenegger, he invites the ex-Nazi president of Austria [Kurt Waldheim] to his wedding with a girl who is of the Kennedy family, a family of Democrats! He has no shame and sense of what is appropriate or decent.

YVES MONTAND, French actor

☆

Katharine Hepburn's film debut came in 1932 with *A Bill of Divorcement,* playing the daughter of John Barrymore. Afterward Hepburn told him, "Thank goodness I don't have to act with you anymore." Barrymore slyed back, "I didn't know you ever had, darling."

☆

At the RKO studios, Hepburn was called "Katharine of Arrogance." Not without reason, as I could tell you—but why bother? I really have nothing to say about Miss Hepburn which you can print.

ESTELLE WINWOOD, actress

☆

Ann Sothern is a lovely person, a fine actress. She has been underrated, but she's lost her sense of self-discipline—she no longer believes in eating on an empty stomach.

BETTE DAVIS, actress

☆

Where else but in America can a poor black boy like Michael Jackson grow up to be a rich white woman?

RED BUTTONS, actor

☆

How did Tinseltown get so ugly? Why is it today's actors look like male hookers? Alec Baldwin, Richard Gere, Kiefer Sutherland . . . they look like they haven't slept for days—except perhaps for money.   **ANTHONY PERKINS,** actor

☆

If Peter O'Toole had been any prettier, it would have been *Florence of Arabia.*

NOEL COWARD, actor, writer, composer

☆

[Bob] Hope is not a comedian. He just translates what others write for him.   **GROUCHO MARX,** actor

☆

Gina Lollobrigida's personality is limited. She is good playing a peasant but is incapable of playing a lady. That said, I don't think she's positively mad about me.

SOPHIA LOREN, actress

☆

I do not talk about Sophia Loren. I do not wish to make for her publicity. She has a talent, but not such a big talent.

GINA LOLLOBRIGIDA, actress

☆

And you can tell Miss Shearer that I didn't get where I am on my ass.

JOAN CRAWFORD with a message for Norma Shearer
[married to her boss, Irving Thalberg]

☆

It was like kissing Hitler.

> **TONY CURTIS,** actor, after filming a scene
> with Marilyn Monroe in *Some Like It Hot*

☆

I have never been a fan of Woody Allen's. I'm sorry.
Somebody closed the door on me there. God knows, many
people say he's the funniest in the world, but I've never been
able to appreciate his humor. I find him neurotic.

> **GEORGE C. SCOTT,** actor

☆

Kathleen Turner's okay in stills. When she talks and
moves about, she reminds me of someone who works in a
supermarket.

> **ANN SOTHERN,** actress

☆

Ingrid Bergman speaks five languages and can't act in
any of them.

> **JOHN GIELGUD,** actor, director

☆

You always knew where you were with Errol Flynn—he
always lets you down.

> **DAVID NIVEN,** actor

☆

No wonder Clara Bow had *It*. She caught It from receiv-
ing too many passes from too many football players.

> **SUSAN HAYWARD,** actress

☆

Doing love scenes with Clark Gable in *Gone With the Wind* was not that romantic. His dentures smelled something awful. **VIVIEN LEIGH,** actress

☆

Wet she's a star, dry she ain't.

JOE PASTERNAK, actor, about
swimming actress Esther Williams

☆

I'm not upset about my divorce from Tom Arnold. I'm only upset I'm not a widow. **ROSEANNE BARR,** actress

☆

She is her biggest fan. If Kathleen Turner had been a man, I would have punched her out long ago.

BURT REYNOLDS, actor

☆

He's the type of man who will end up dying in his own arms. **MAMIE VAN DOREN,** actress,
regarding Warren Beatty, actor

☆

Joan always cried a lot. Her tear ducts must be close to her bladder. **BETTE DAVIS,** actress, regarding
Joan Crawford, actress

☆

Hedda Hopper and Louella Parsons [Hollywood columnists]. They were bitches.

ELIZABETH TAYLOR, actress

☆

Go figure those two. Hedda Hopper was homophobic, and her only child was homosexual. Louella was anti-Semitic, yet she was born Jewish, then converted. They were a demented pair, and Hollywood was even more demented for allowing them so much power over people's careers and lives.

GALE SONDERGAARD, actress

☆

Mr. Dean appears to be wearing my last year's wardrobe and using my last year's talent.

MARLON BRANDO, actor, in 1955,
regarding James Dean.

☆

Garbo had this androgynous quality. If she'd been American, I think the ladies in the audience would have thought her sort of dykey.

GALE SONDERGAARD, actress

☆

An actor's a guy who, if you ain't talking about him, ain't listening.

MARLON BRANDO, actor

☆

Bette and I are very good friends. There's nothing I wouldn't say to her face—both of them.

> **TALLULAH BANKHEAD,** actress
> about Bette Davis, actress

☆

I *acted* vulgar. Madonna *is* vulgar.

> **MARLENE DIETRICH,** actress

☆

That broad's got a great future behind her. . . .

> **CONSTANCE BENNETT,** actress, on newcomer
> Marilyn Monroe, actress

☆

She's jumped right into the movie game, but I think people should learn to act first.

> **ROSEANNE BARR,** comedienne, actress, regarding
> Madonna's role in *Desperately Seeking Susan* (1985)

☆

Well at least he has finally found his true love. What a pity he can't marry himself.

> **FRANK SINATRA,** singer, actor,
> regarding Robert Redford, actor

☆

Dramatic art, in her opinion, is knowing how to fill a sweater.

> **BETTE DAVIS,** actress,
> regarding Jayne Mansfield, actress

☆

It's a new low for actresses when you have to wonder what's between her ears instead of her legs.

KATHARINE HEPBURN, actress,
regarding Sharon Stone, actress

☆

[Bob Hope] is an applause junkie. Instead of growing old gracefully and doing something with his money, all he does is have an anniversary with the President looking on. He's a pathetic guy. **MARLON BRANDO,** actor

☆

Tallulah was sitting with a group of people, giving the monologue she always thought was conversation.

ZOE CALDWELL, actress

☆

I never forget a face, but in your case I'll make an exception. **GROUCHO MARX,** actor, comedian

☆

When *Mary of Scotland* (1936) was being filmed, Queen Elizabeth was played by Florence Eldridge, and Katharine had the title role. But Hepburn wanted to play both roles, and she kept yapping and yapping until the whole cast was fed up. Finally, John Carradine confronted her: "If you played both parts, how would you know which queen to upstage?"

☆

Claudette Colbert kept forgetting her lines, and tempers were hot. Miss Colbert apologized, "I knew these lines backward last night," to which Noel Coward shot back, "And that's the way you're saying them this morning."

☆

I married a designer [Oleg Cassini]. The thing is, I wasn't the only person he had designs on.

GENE TIERNEY, actress

☆

I am free of all prejudices. I hate every one equally.

W. C. FIELDS, unique comic actor, writer, juggler

☆

The son of a bitch is a ballet dancer! He's the best ballet dancer that ever lived, and if I get a good chance, I'll strangle him with my bare hands.

W. C. FIELDS, unique comic actor, writer, juggler
after viewing a Charlie Chaplin movie

☆

Sheesh! I'd hate to have his nerve in my tooth.

LUCILLE BALL'S view of Orson Welles, director, actor

☆

Ricardo Montalban is to improvisational acting what Mount Rushmore is to animation.

JOHN CASSAVETES, actor

☆

It's hard to believe Anna Magnani won the Academy Award and not Susan Hayward! Shouldn't they have separate categories for foreigners? I mean, they're called the Oscars, not the Raviolis.

WARD BOND, actor

☆

Don Ameche got an award for break-dancing in *Cocoon,* only all his dancing was done by a stunt double. Doesn't the dancer deserve his own junior Oscar?

JAMES COCO, actor

☆

Hollywood's dumbest blonde never even made a Hollywood picture. It is Brigitte Bardot. She is—she was—beautiful in an overripe way. But she was and remains cheap, petty, jealous, bigoted, and untalented. She also tries to kill herself every few years without success. I hope she never succeeds, but one wonders if she is very good at anything?

YVES MONTAND, French actor

☆

You know, once they're dead, death just scrubs [celebrities] clean. Everybody says, "Oh, they were wonderful." Suddenly, Grace Kelly didn't drink.

JOAN RIVERS, comedienne

☆

She's the original good time that was had by all.

BETTE DAVIS, actress on
starlet Marilyn Monroe

☆

It must be tough having a beautiful mother like Cher and being named Chastity. I guess the only thing worse would be being beautiful and being named Slut.

AVA GARDNER, actress

Orson Welles Summed It Up Ruefully

Every actor in his heart believes everything
bad that's printed about him.

Samuel Goldwyn, a King of Producers
(The Lord of Apocrypha)

Anyone who sees a psychiatrist
should have his head examined.

Samuel Goldfish (approximately) was born into a poor family in Warsaw on August 7, 1882. Orphaned early, he waved *do widzenia* to Poland and crossed the Atlantic, arriving in New York in 1896 at age fourteen, with a name so infested with consonants that *Goldfish* was the nearest pronunciation the Ellis Island clerk could come up with.

By the time he died in California at age ninety-one (his name long before changed to Goldwyn), he was a motion picture colossus who had enriched America's culture and society.

As the immigrant boy, he sold gloves in upstate New York, saved his money, and went west to get in on the emerging movie industry. A smart, irascible, difficult egoist, he made his way quickly, and by 1923 he was an important independent producer. The key word was *independent.* "When you have a partner, you don't need an enemy," he said.

Samuel Goldwyn was a perfectionist with a volcanic temper. He knew what he wanted when he wanted it, and he wanted the best. Once established, he hired the finest writers he could find. He even had the *chutzpah* to offer movie contracts to George Bernard Shaw and Sigmund Freud.

He worshiped at the altar of talent. Then he altered the talent. "He screamed at them, beat them to a frazzle, argued with them, and praised them when he got the picture he wanted." The writer Ben Hecht said Goldwyn dealt with creative people like "an irritated man shaking a slot machine."

But consider the results:

Wuthering Heights, The Pride of the Yankees, Arrowsmith, Dodsworth, Stella Dallas, Dead End, The Westerner, The Little Foxes, and *The Best Years of Our Lives,* winner of the 1946 Academy Award for Best Picture. He was so proud of it that he proclaimed, "I don't care if the picture makes a nickel. I just want every man, woman, and child in America to see it."

His immaculate productions of good taste and high quality, produced on a grand scale, were praised for having "that Goldwyn touch."

I'll tell you what else had "that Goldwyn touch": English. After he got through with it.

So much of his speech was merrily mangled that his remarks were savored, passed around, and collected as "Goldwynisms." Many are genuine. Some are aprocraphyl. All are as delightful as are the remarks of Mrs. Malaprop (created by Richard Sheridan in 1775). It was she who said, "He is the very pineapple of politeness."

When an aide suggested that a screenplay was too caustic, Goldwyn said, "Who cares about the expense?"

But while making another movie, he ordered his staff to "spare no expense to make everything as economical as possible."

In 1934, when Goldwyn sought the movie rights to Lillian Hellman's Broadway hit *The Children's Hour*, a staffer protested: "Mr. Goldwyn, you can't buy that property. It's about lesbians." Goldwyn shrugged: "So we'll make them Albanians."

He made that one into a hit in 1936, retitled *These Three*, with neither Albanians *nor* lesbians. When its director William Wellman switched one night scene to daylight, Goldwyn stormed at him: "Nobody can change night into day, or vice versa, without asking me first."

When James Thurber complained that the adaptation of his fantasy *The Secret Life of Walter Mitty* was too violent, Goldwyn attempted to soothe him: "I'm sorry you felt it was too blood and thirsty."

Thurber replied, "Not only did I think so, but I was horror and struck."

I had a great idea this morning, but I didn't like it.

What we want is a story that starts with an earthquake and works its way up to a climax.

Informed that some more Indians were needed as extras for a Western, Goldwyn had the solution: "Get some more from the reservoir."

After a preview: "It will create an excitement that will sweep the country like wildflowers."

Defensive about a flop: "Go see it and see for yourself why you shouldn't see it."

To a writer: "Let's have some new clichés."

And again: "Let's bring it up to date with some snappy nineteenth-century dialogue."

Cryptic: "It's more than magnificent—it's mediocre."

Fatalistic: "If people don't want to go to a picture, nobody can stop them."

During a story conference: "I read part of the book all the way through."

Dismissive: "I don't pay any attention to him. I don't even ignore him."

Inviting differing opinions: "I don't want any yes-men around me. I want everybody to tell me the truth even if it costs them their jobs!"

To the author Sidney Kingsley: "If you don't disagree with me, how will I know I'm right?"

To an assistant: "I challenge you to give me a frank, affirmative answer: yes or no."

Problems? No problem: "I don't care about that; it rolls off my back like a duck."

Irritated: "That makes me so sore it gets my dandruff up."

Decisive: "I'll give you a definite maybe."

Goldwyn, when partly complimentary: "You are partly one hundred percent right."

Goldwyn, when biwordly adamant: "I can answer you in two words. Im Possible."

Declining a risk: "I would be sticking my head in a moose."

Movies are a tough game: "It's dog eat dog, and nobody's going to eat me."

On his guard: "Directors are always biting the hand that lays the golden egg."

Signing out loud: "A verbal contract isn't worth the paper it's written on."

Archives: "We've got twenty-five years' worth of files out there, just sitting around. Now what I want you to do is go out there and throw everything out—but make a copy of everything first."

Politics: "If Roosevelt was alive he'd turn in his grave."

Personal lifestyles: "He's living beyond his means, but he can afford it."

When the producer Arthur Hornblow Jr. told him that his newborn son would also be named Arthur: "But why *Arthur*? Every Tom, Dick and Harry is called Arthur."

Crisis: "I felt like we were on the brink of the abscess." According to the *New York Times,* this may be the earliest known Goldwynism.

Rebuttal: "There's not a single word of untruth in that."

His proposed slogan: "Goldwyn pictures griddle the earth."

Sculpture: "My wife's hands are so beautiful, I'm having a bust made of them."

To a screenwriter adapting his own work: "Here I am paying you big money to rewrite your script, and what for? All you do is change the words."

Who should know better?: "They didn't release that movie; it escaped."

On the funeral of his rival, Louis B. Mayer: "The only reason so many people showed up at his funeral was because they wanted to make sure he was dead."

Technology: "A wide screen just makes a bad film twice as bad."

On reading the synopsis of a story by the symbolist Maurice Maeterlinck: "My God . . . The hero is a bee! That Morrie, I trusted him, and he wrote me a story about bees."

As the years go by: "We have passed a lot of water since then."

Business: "If I was in this business for the business, I wouldn't be in this business!"

His life: "I'm never going to write my autobiography as long as I live."

Trust: "If you can't give me your word of honor, will you give me your promise?"

The sage: "Why should people go out and pay money to see bad films when they can stay at home and see bad television for nothing?"

The Office Meeting

GOLDWYN: "We've got to get some new blood around here. I want to sign up a young writer, talented but completely unknown, who'll bring us new ideas and a fresh viewpoint."

MIRIAM HOWELL (GOLDWYN'S AIDE): "I know just the man. A young playwright named John Patrick."

GOLDWYN: "Never heard of him. Who else can you come up with?"

Garson Kanin, the prolific writer and husband of actress Ruth Gordon, told Gene Shalit, with great excitement, that he himself, with his own ears, was present when an original Goldwynism occurred. Kanin had been invited to California to discuss a script, and Goldwyn started their interview by saying, "I hear you're a very smart genius."

Goldwyn was visiting a friend in Connecticut. The friend had just installed a sundial in his garden.

"What's that?" asked Goldwyn.

"It's a sundial."

"What does it do?"

"It uses the shadow from the sun to tell roughly what time it is. See—here is noon; here, say, it's three o'clock, and so on."

"My goodness!" said Goldwyn. "What will they think up next?"

PRODUCTION ASSISTANT: "But, Mr. Goldwyn, you said you wanted a spectacle."

GOLDWYN: "Yes, but goddam it, I wanted an intimate spectacle!"

The trouble with this business is the dearth of bad pictures.

I was always an independent, even when I had partners.

Our comedies are not to be laughed at.

Samuel Goldwyn: A Summing Up

"I was a rebel, a lone wolf. My pictures were my own. I financed them myself and answered solely to myself. My mistakes and my successes were my own. My one rule was to please myself, and if I did that, there was a good chance I would please others."

Groucho Lays Down the Law . . . yers

In 1946, when the Marx Brothers planned a movie called *A Night in Casablanca,* Warner Bros. threatened legal action because, five years earlier, their film called *Casablanca* had become a classic, having won Academy Awards for best picture, best director, and best original screenplay. Groucho, representing his brothers and himself, immediately dispatched the following letter:

Dear Warner Brothers:

Apparently there is more than one way of conquering a city and holding it as your own. For example, up to the time that we contemplated making this picture, I had no idea that the city of Casablanca belonged exclusively to Warner Brothers. However, it was only a few days after our announcement appeared that we received your long, ominous legal document warning us not the use the name Casablanca.

It seems that in 1471, Ferdinand Balboa Warner, your great-great-grandfather, while looking for a shortcut to the city of Burbank, had stumbled on the shores of Africa and, raising his alpenstock (which he later turned in for a hundred shares of common), named it Casablanca.

I just don't understand your attitude. Even if you plan on rereleasing your picture, I am sure the average movie fan could learn in time to distinguish between Ingrid Bergman and Harpo. I don't know whether I could, but I certainly would like to try.

You claim you own Casablanca and that no one else can use that name without your permission. What about "Warner Brothers"? Do you own that, too. You probably have a right to use the name Warner, but what about Brothers? Professionally, we were brothers long before you were. We were touring the sticks as The Marx Brothers when Vitaphone was still a gleam in the inventor's eye, and even before us there had been other brothers—the Smith brothers; the brothers Karamazov; Dan Brothers, an outfielder with Detroit, and "Brother, Can You Spare a Dime?" This was originally "Brothers, Can You Spare a Dime?" but this was spreading a dime pretty thin, so they threw out one brother, gave all the money to the other brother, and whittled it down to, "Brother, Can You Spare a Dime?"

Now Jack, how about you? Do you maintain that yours is an original name? Well, it's not. It was used long before you were born. Offhand, I can think of two Jacks—there was Jack of "Jack and the Beanstalk," and Jack the Ripper, who cut quite a figure in his day.

As for you, Harry, you probably sign your checks sure in the belief that you are the first Harry of all time and that all the other Harrys are impostors. I can think of two Harrys that preceded you. There was Lighthorse Harry of Revolutionary fame and a Harry Applebaum who lived on the corner of 93rd Street and Lexington Avenue. Unfortunately, Applebaum wasn't too well known. The last I heard of him, he was selling neckties at Weber and Heilbroner.

Now about the Burbank studio. I believe this is what you brothers call your place. Old man Burbank is gone. Perhaps you remember him. He was a great man in a garden. His wife often said Luther had ten green thumbs. What a witty woman she must have been! Burbank was the wizard who crossed all those fruits and vegetables until he had all the plants in such a confused and jittery condition that they could never decide whether to enter the dining room on the meat platter or the dessert dish.

This is pure conjecture, of course, but who knows—perhaps Burbank's survivors aren't too happy with the fact that a plant that grinds out pictures on a quota settled in their town, appropriated Burbank's name and uses it as a front for the films. It is even possible that the Burbank family is prouder of the potato produced by the old man than they are of the fact that from your studio emerged "Casablanca" or even "Gold Diggers of 1931."

This all seems to add up to a pretty bitter tirade, but I assure you it's not meant to. I love Warners. Some of my best friends are Warner Brothers. It is even possible that I am doing you an injustice and that you, yourselves, know nothing at all about this dog-in-the-Wanger attitude. It wouldn't surprise me at all to discover that the heads of your legal department are unaware of this absurd dispute, for I am acquainted with many of them and they are fine fellows with curly black hair, double-breasted suits, and a love of their fellow man that out-Saroyans Saroyan.

I have a hunch that this attempt to prevent us from using the title is the brainchild of some ferret-faced shyster, serving a brief apprenticeship in your legal department. I know the type well—hot out of law school, hungry for success, and too ambitious to follow the natural laws of promotion. This bar sinister probably needled your attorneys, most of whom are fine fellows with curly black hair, double-breasted suits, etc., into attempting to enjoin us. Well, he won't get away with it! We'll fight him to the highest court! No pasty-faced legal adventurer is going to cause bad blood between the Warners and the Marxes. We are all brothers under the skin and we'll remain friends till the last reel of "A Night in Casablanca" goes tumbling over the spool.

Sincerely,

Groucho Marx

For some curious reason, this letter seemed to puzzle the Warner Bros. legal department. They wrote—in all seriousness—and asked if the Marxes could give them some idea of what their story was about. They felt something might be worked out. So Groucho replied:

Dear Warners:

There isn't much I can tell you about the story. In it I play a Doctor of Divinity who ministers to the natives and, as a sideline, hawks can openers and pea jackets to the savages along the Gold Coast of Africa.

When I first meet Chico, he is working in a saloon, selling sponges to barflies who are unable to carry their liquor. Harpo is an Arabian caddie who lives in a small Grecian urn on the outskirts of the city.

As the picture opens, Porridge, a mealy-mouthed native girl, is sharpening some arrows for the hunt. Paul Hangover, our hero, is constantly lighting two cigarettes simultaneously. He apparently is unaware of the cigarette shortage.

There are many scenes of splendor and fierce antagonisms, and Color, an Abyssinian messenger boy, runs Riot. Riot, in case you have never been there, is a small nightclub at the edge of town.

There's a lot more I could tell you, but I don't

want to spoil it for you. All this has been okayed by the Hays office, Good Housekeeping, and the survivors of the Haymarket Riots; and if the times are ripe, this picture can be the opening gun in a new worldwide disaster.

Cordially,

Groucho Marx

Instead of mollifying them, this note seemed to puzzle the attorneys even more; they wrote back and said they still didn't understand the story line and would appreciate it if Mr. Marx would explain the plot in more detail. So Groucho obliged with the following:

Dear Brothers:

Since I last wrote you, I regret to say there have been some changes in the plot of our new picture, "A Night in Casablanca." In the new version I play Bordello, the sweetheart of Humphrey Bogart. Harpo and Chico are itinerant rug peddlers who weary of laying rugs and enter a monastery just for a lark. This is a good joke on them, as there hasn't been a lark in the place for fifteen years.

Across from this monastery, hard by a jetty, is a waterfront hotel, chockfull of apple-cheeked damsels, most of whom have been barred by the Hays Office for soliciting. In the fifth reel, Gladstone makes a speech that sets the House of Commons in an uproar and the King promptly asks for his resignation. Harpo marries a hotel detective; Chico operates an Ostrich farm.

Humphrey Bogart's girl, Bordello, spends her last years in a Bacall house.

This, as you can see, is a very skimpy outline. The only thing that can save us from extinction is a continuation of the film shortage.

Fondly,

Groucho Marx

After that, Groucho heard no more from Warner Bros.' legal department.

Writers, Producers, & Directors Take On The Stars

Actors and actresses on the screen speak (the lines of writers) and do (what the director tells them to do). Fans may think that the glamorous Sis Boombah is a witty woman, when she's merely mouthing the writer's words, and almost every move she makes is the director's vision. There are exceptions, but that's the general situation. What writers, directors, and producers and the critics think of the famous screen stars they often work with is not always admirable. Here's a sampling of piercing **POT SHOTS.**

☆

The question is whether Marilyn [Monroe] is a person at all, or one of the greatest Dupont products ever invented.

She has breasts like granite and a brain like Swiss cheese, full of holes.

BILLY WILDER, director, writer

☆

Lana Turner couldn't act her way out of her form-fitting cashmeres.

TENNESSEE WILLIAMS, writer

☆

Overweight, overbosomed, overpaid, and undertalented.

DAVID SUSSKIND, producer, describing
Elizabeth Taylor, actress

☆

There are times when Richard Gere has the warm effect of a wind tunnel at dawn, waiting for work, all sheen, inner curve, and posed emptiness.

DAVID THOMSON, writer, in
A Biographical Dictionary of Film (1994)

☆

When the celebrated humorist S. J. Perelman arrived in Hollywood to write for the Marx Brothers, Herman Mankiewitz, who had labored on their movies, warned him: "They're mercurial, devious, and ungrateful. I hate to depress you, but you'll rue the day you ever took the assignment. This is an ordeal by fire. Make sure you wear asbestos pants."

HERMAN MANKIEWITZ, writer, producer,
warning S. J. Perelman, writer

☆

From 1933 to 1939 [Fred Astaire and Ginger Rogers] did nine pictures for me. Overnight they became one of the hottest box office attractions in the industry. But I've never known two people who wanted to be further apart. It was a constant struggle.　　　**PANDRO S. BERMAN,** producer

☆

Sandy Dennis has made an acting style out of postnasal drip.　　　**PAULINE KAEL,** critic

☆

She has only two things going for her—a father and a mother.　　　**JOHN SIMON,** critic, describing Liza Minnelli, daughter of Judy Garland and the director Vincente Minnelli

☆

[Barbra Streisand] is a real "kvetch"—she's always moaning about something or other: a really hard-to-please lady. But I can handle that. When she's "kvetching" I simply say: "Shut up and give me a little kiss, will ya, huh?" or "Stick out your boobs, they're beautiful." And after that she's fine for the next ten minutes.　　　**PETER BOGDANOVICH,** director

☆

Miss Garland's figure resembles the giant-economy-size tube of toothpaste in girls' bathrooms. Squeezed intemperately at all points, it acquires a shape that defies definition by the most resourceful solid geometrician.

JOHN SIMON, critic, on Judy Garland, singer, actress

☆

Merle Oberon speaks eighteen languages and can't say no in any of them.   **DOROTHY PARKER,** writer

☆

The queen of sequential monogamy.

> **ARIANNA HUFFINGTON,** about actress
> Elizabeth Taylor (married eight times)

☆

She was a gigantic pain in the ass. She demonstrated certifiable proof on insanity.

> **ROMAN POLANSKI,** after directing
> Faye Dunaway in *Chinatown* (1974)

☆

Listen, dearie. I was at the top when you were a has-been practicing to be a never-was.

> **LOUELLA PARSONS,** knocking rival
> gossip columnist Hedda Hopper

☆

Take one black widow spider, cross it with a scorpion, wean their poisonous offspring on a mixture of prussic acid and treacle, and you'll get the honeyed sting of Hedda Hopper.   **ANONYMOUS**

☆

Directing Marilyn Monroe was like directing Lassie. You needed fourteen takes to get one right.

OTTO PREMINGER, director

☆

The closest thing to Roseanne Barr's singing the national anthem was my cat being neutered.

JOHNNY CARSON, comedian

☆

I love my job, and, with the exception of Kim Basinger, most of the people I work with.

JEFFREY KATZENBURG, motion picture executive

☆

I'd give it up, if I could have back the nine months of my life I spent with Dustin making it.

SYDNEY POLLACK, speaking of his Oscar nomination as best director for *Tootsie,* starring Dustin Hoffman.

☆

The insufferably smug and woodchuck-cheeked Minnie Driver proffers what the French call a *tête à gifler*—a face begging to be slapped. **JOHN SIMON,** critic

☆

A day away from Tallulah Bankhead is like a month in the country. **HOWARD DIETZ,** writer

☆

Richard Gere and Cindy Crawford: What a concept—his body's by Nautilus and her mind's by Mattel.

SAM KINISON, composer, comedian

☆

Kevin Costner . . . throughout the movie, displays the sensitivity and eloquence of a pizza delivery man.

JOHN SIMON, critic

☆

My God, Edna, you look almost like a man.

> **NOEL COWARD,** actor-writer, to Edna Ferber, author, whose books became movies, and who was wearing a suit

So do you.   **EDNA FERBER** replying

☆

Marilyn was mean. Terribly mean. The meanest woman I have ever met around this town. I have never met anybody as mean as Marilyn Monroe or as utterly fabulous on the screen.   **BILLY WILDER,** Marilyn's director
in *Some Like It Hot*

☆

She has no charm, delicacy, or taste. She's just an arrogant little tail-twitcher who's learned to throw sex in your face.

NUNNALLY JOHNSON, writer,
on Marilyn Monroe, actress

☆

Keir Dullea, gone tomorrow.

NOEL COWARD, actor, writer,
on the *Space Odyssey* actor

☆

PROSPECTIVE GUEST: "I really can't come to your party. I can't bear fools."

DOROTHY PARKER: "That's strange, your mother could."

☆

A vacuum with nipples.

MARILYN MONROE, actress, described by
Otto Preminger, director

☆

Studio heads have foreheads by dint of electrolysis.

S. J. PERELMAN, writer

☆

Clark Gable's ears make him look like a taxicab with both doors open. **HOWARD HUGHES,** producer

☆

Peter O'Toole looks like he's walking around just to save the funeral expenses. **JOHN HUSTON,** director

☆

The T is silent, as in Harlow.

> **MARGOT ASQUITH,** socialite, wit, and wife of
> British prime minister (1908–16) to
> Jean Harlow, American actress, who
> mispernounced Asquith's first name

☆

[Greta Garbo] is hermaphroditic, with the cold quality
of a mermaid. **TENNESSEE WILLIAMS,** writer

☆

There but for the grace of God goes God.

> **HERMAN MANKIEWICZ** on Orson Welles
> (coauthors of *Citizen Kane*)

Jack Warner

(Oh, Brother!)

An empty taxi stopped, and Jack Warner got out.
Many have taken credit

Jack Warner (1892–1978) reigned over Hollywood's movie parade longer than did any other movie mogul. Jack, Sam, Harry, and Al were the Warner Brothers, and their studio introduced such stars as Bette Davis, Jimmy Cagney, Errol Flynn, Doris Day, Humphrey Bogart, Lauren Bacall, Bugs Bunny, and Daffy Duck.

Brothers they were, but Jack was the production boss. Three of his movies won Best Picture Oscars—*Casablanca, My Fair Lady,* and *The Life of Emile Zola,* starring Paul Muni, who was, as usual, unrecognizable in his elaborate makeup. "Why are we paying Muni so much money when we can't find him?" Warner once cracked to Bette Davis.

Warner was a risk taker with a reputation for picking

future winners. His studio is credited with pioneering sound; 1927's historic *The Jazz Singer,* written by Samson Raphaelson, was a Warner picture.

Again and again Jack dazzled the public with now-classic musicals: (*42nd Street* in 1933), thrilled them with now-classic gangster pictures (*Little Caesar* in 1930), and later the studio enthusiastically backed color.

Those are facts. For opinions, one might start with Wilson Mizner: "If Jack Warner had oilcloth pockets, he'd steal soup."

☆

David Brown, the honored producer of such triumphs as *The Verdict, Jaws,* and *The Player,* and author of *Let Me Entertain You* and the witty *Brown's Guide to Growing Gray,* recalls the infamous 1950s political Blacklist that barred many writers, directors, and actors from working in Hollywood. The studios denied that such a list existed. When a certain director accused Warner of not hiring him because of it, Warner said, "There is no Blacklist, and you're not on it."

☆

A pair of Warners' most successful screenwriters were also brothers, Julius and Philip Epstein. A time came when the studio instituted a strict nine-to-five time clock workday for all employees. Creative people like the Epsteins were furious. Warner called them in for a stern talk. "Executives can come in at nine," he said, "railroad presidents can come in at nine, bank presidents can come in at nine, why the hell can't *you* come in at nine?"

A week or so later, the Epsteins delivered the first thirty pages of their new screenplay. Attached was a note: *"Dear J. L. Have the bank president finish the script."*

☆

When Albert Einstein visited Hollywood, celebrities vied for invitations to the lavish party that was caused for the physicist whose theory of relativity was known by many but understood by few. During the evening the great scientist was introduced to Jack Warner, who told him, "I have my own theory of relatives. Don't hire 'em."

☆

Unlike Sam Goldwyn, who revered good writers, Jack Warner had his own definition: "A schmuck with a typewriter."

☆

At a production meeting to discuss possible subjects for a film, Jack Warner said: "Anything but Beethoven. Nobody wants to see a movie about a blind composer."

☆

It's our fault. We should have given him better parts.

     JACK WARNER's reaction to Ronald Reagan
     being elected governor of California

When a story or wisecrack travels from one person to another, it may be embellished, condensed, swollen—but if it's good it will endure. My friend and neighbor, the distinguished actress Maureen Stapleton, told me how a Hollywood happenstance was just happenstanced enough to alter its tone. She said it was okay to tell the whole story, and urged me to add that, "Maureen regards Ann-Margret with the utmost esteem." Which is also how I regard Maureen. Here it is:

In 1962, I went to Hollywood to appear in the screen version of the hit Broadway musical *Bye Bye Birdie.* Although I was still in my thirties, I was cast as Dick Van Dyke's mother. Like Beulah Bondi before me, I portrayed older ladies throughout my younger life. Allegedly, at a wrap-up party for the cast and crew of *Bye Bye Birdie,* the producer got up and told everyone he was thrilled to be associated with such a superb film and so many fabulous people, especially Ann-Margret, the singing-dancing ingenue. The director then rose, paid tribute to the company and ended by saying he, too, was thrilled to work with Ann-Margret. Next, Dick Van Dyke got up, praised everyone and finished by, once again, singling out Ann-Margret. Finally, I stood up and said, "Well, it looks like I'm the only one on this picture who didn't try to fuck Ann-Margret."

I hate to disillusion anyone, but that's not what happened. Actually, we were at a party at somebody's home, and I noticed that Ann-Margret was sitting on a couch surrounded by a bunch of guys coming on to her. About an hour later she was in the same place. I was on my way to the buffet table and called over to her. "Annie, why don't you come and sit with me? I'm the only one here who doesn't want to fuck you."

That's the true story, and I wouldn't care how it was told except that I like Ann-Margret and the first version makes it sound like I was putting her down. Much later, I was back in Hollywood and ran into Ann-Margret, whom I hadn't seen since *Birdie*. I repeated the screwed-up account of the party. "Honey," I apologized at the end, "I'm gonna get this thing straightened out if it's the last thing I do." Annie smiled, patted my hand, and said, "Leave the story alone, Maureen, it's a classic."

☆

Y'Don't Say—1

WILLIAM POWELL: "I'm a hero. I was shot two times in the *Tribune*."

MYRNA LOY: "I read you were shot five times in the tabloids."

WILLIAM POWELL: "It's not true. He didn't come anywhere near my tabloids."

> *The Thin Man* (1934): screenplay by Albert Hackett,
> Dashiell Hammett; directed by W. S. Van Dyke

☆

If a thing is worth doing, it is worth doing slowly . . . very slowly.

GYPSY ROSE LEE, celebrated ecdysiast turned writer

☆

Asked if Smokey the Bear had left a widow, the actor Paul Lynde said, "Let's just say that at the services, they had to sedate Ranger Bob."

☆

If I'd been a ranch they would've called me the bar nothing.
RITA HAYWORTH in *Gilda* (1946): screenplay by
Marion Parsonnet; directed by Charles Vidor

☆

Every man I've known has fallen in love with Gilda and wakened with me.   **RITA HAYWORTH,** actress, referring to her
glamorous sexy role as *Gilda* (1946)

☆

Old Cary Grant fine. How you?
CARY GRANT in reply to a telegram asking
"HOW OLD CARY GRANT?"

☆

From birth to age eighteen, a girl needs good parents. From eighteen to thirty-five, she needs good looks. From thirty-five to fifty-five, she needs a good personality. From fifty-five on, she needs good cash.
SOPHIE TUCKER, "The Last of The Red
Hot Mamas," said at age sixty-nine

☆

AUDREY HEPBURN: "I already know an awful lot of people, and until one of them dies, I couldn't possibly meet anyone else."

CARY GRANT: "Well, if anyone goes on the critical list, let me know."

> *Charade* (1963): screenplay by Peter Stone and
> Marc Behm; directed by Stanley Donnen

☆

State of affairs? What state of affairs? I haven't had an affair for some time.

> **MARLENE DIETRICH,** as Catherine the Great in
> *The Scarlet Empress* (1934): screenplay by Manuel
> Komroff; directed by Josef von Sternberg

☆

Ingrid, Ingrid, Ingrid! Whatever got into you?

> **LOUELLA PARSONS,** gossip columnist on radio
> when Ingrid Bergman's affair with director
> Roberto Rossellini resulted in her pregnancy

☆

He'll regret it to his dying day—if ever he lives that long.

> **VICTOR MCLAGLEN** about John Wayne in
> *The Quiet Man* (1952): screenplay by
> Frank Nugent; directed by John Ford

☆

I'd love to kiss you, but I just washed my hair.

> **BETTE DAVIS** in *Cabin in the Cotton* (1932):
> screenplay by Paul Green; directed by
> Michael Curtiz (Miss Davis said this was
> her favorite line)

☆

I don't care what is written about me so long as it isn't true.

> **KATHARINE HEPBURN,** actress

☆

The embarrassing thing is that the salad dressing is out-grossing my films.

> **PAUL NEWMAN,** actor, on his food products
> (all profits go to charity with more than
> $100 million by the start of 2003)

☆

Too bad that all the people who know how to run the country are busy driving taxicabs and cutting hair.

> **GEORGE BURNS,** comedian, actor

☆

Same old story. Boy finds girl. Boy loses girl. Girl finds boy. Boy forgets girl. Boy remembers girl. Girl dies in a tragic blimp accident over the Orange Bowl on New Year's Day.

> **LESLIE NEILSEN:** In *The Naked Gun* (1988):
> screenplay by Jerry Zucker, Jim Abrahams,
> David Zucker, Pat Proft; directed by
> David Zucker

☆

Oh, I love sitting on your lap. I could sit here all day if you didn't stand up.

> **GROUCHO MARX** to Thelma Todd in *Horsefeathers*
> (1932): screenplay by Bert Kalmar, Harry Ruby,
> S. J. Perelman; directed by Norman Z. McLeod

☆

Then she tried to sit on my lap while I was standing up.

> **HUMPHREY BOGART** to Charles D. Brown (the
> butler) in *The Big Sleep* (1946): screenplay by
> William Faulkner, Jules Furthman, Leigh
> Bracket; directed by Howard Hawks

☆

This is just a personal opinion, but I don't think any other star got to deliver as many memorable dialogue lines as did Humphrey Bogart. With Gary Cooper we think "Yup." Gable got the famous "Frankly, my dear, I don't give a damn." Brando had "I could have been a contender," and Spencer Tracy—I can't come up with a single line to associate with that great actor.

> **WILLIAM GOLDMAN,** Oscar-winning screenwriter

☆

ELDERLY LADY PASSENGER SITTING NEXT TO ROBERT
    HAYS AS PLANE IS ABOUT TAKE OFF: "Nervous?"
ROBERT HAYS: "Yes."

OLD LADY: "First time?"

ROBERT HAYS: "No, I've been nervous lots of times."

> *Airplane* (1980): screenplay by Jim Abrahams, David
> Zucker, Jerry Zucker; directed by Jim Abrahams

☆

The two most beautiful words in the English language are *"Check Enclosed."* **DOROTHY PARKER,** writer

☆

Was "1" a good year?

> **ZERO MOSTEL,** checking a wine label in *A Funny
> Thing Happened on the Way to the Forum* (1966):
> screenplay by Melvin Frank and Michael
> Pertwee; directed by Richard Lester

☆

DUDLEY MOORE: "I'm going to take a bath."

JOHN GIELGUD (AS HIS BUTLER): "I'll alert the media."

> **ARTHUR** (1981), written and directed
> by Steve Gordon

☆

Love is something that goes on between a man and a .45 that won't jam.

> **ALAN LADD** in *Appointment with Danger* (1951),
> directed by Lewis Allen

☆

VIVIAN BLAINE: "The doctor thinks that my cold might be caused by psychology."

FRANK SINATRA: "Nah. How does he know you got psychology?"

> *Guys and Dolls* (1955), written and directed
> by Joseph L. Mankiewicz

☆

He's the kind of guy that, when he dies, he's going up to heaven and give God a hard time for making him bald.

> **MARLON BRANDO,** actor,
> on Frank Sinatra, singer, actor

☆

Isn't it strange how that lovely song reminds you of chicken salad?

> **JOAN CRAWFORD** to Cliff Robertson in *Autumn
> Leaves* (1956): screenplay by Jean Rouverol,
> Hugo Butler, Lewis Meltzer, Robert Blees;
> directed by Richard Aldrich

☆

Is my husband in your chickenlike arms?

> **ELIZABETH TAYLOR,** actress, telephoning Susannah
> York in *X, Y, and Zee* (1972): screenplay by
> Edna O'Brien; directed by Brian G. Hutton

☆

I've never been able to understand why, when there's so much space in the world, people should deliberately choose to live in the Middle West.

> **CLIFTON WEBB** in *The Razor's Edge* (1946): written by Lamar Trotti; directed by Edmund Golding

☆

Take it from me, baby, in America nothing fails like success. **BUDD SCHULBERG,** producer

☆

KATHARINE HEPBURN: "Why certainly you must have heard of Hamlet?"

EVE ARDEN: "Well, I meet so many people."

> *Stage Door* (1937): screenplay by Morris Ryskind and Anthony Veiller; directed by Gregory La Cava

☆

JOHN BARRYMORE: "You should play Hamlet."

JIMMY DURANTE: "No, I don't like playing those small towns." *Hollywood Party* (1934)

☆

What he did to Shakespeare, we are doing now to Poland. **SIG RUMAN**, playing a Nazi, commenting on Jack Benny's performance as Hamlet in *To Be or Not to Be* (1942): screenplay by Edwin Justus Mayer, Ernst Lubitsch, Melchior Lengvel; directed by Ernst Lubitsch

☆

George Burns (as God): "You want a miracle? Make a fish from scratch. You can't. You think only God can make a tree? Try coming up with a mackerel."

> *Oh, God!* (1977): screenplay by Larry Gelbart;
> directed by Carl Reiner

☆

Phyllis Povah: "Watercress! I'd just as soon eat my way across a front lawn."

> *The Women* (1939): screenplay by Anita Loos
> from the Claire Boothe Luce stage play;
> directed by George Cukor

☆

I like the way you express yourself, too, you know. It's pithy, yet degenerate.

> **WOODY ALLEN** to Diane Keaton in *Manhattan*
> (1979): screenplay by Woody Allen and
> Marshall Brickman; directed by Woody Allen

☆

Mr. President, I'm not saying we wouldn't get our hair mussed, but I do say not more than ten or twenty million killed, tops, depending on the breaks.

> **GEORGE C. SCOTT** to Peter Sellers in *Dr. Strangelove,*
> *or How I Learned to Stop Worrying and Love the Bomb*
> (1964): screenplay by Terry Southern, Peter George,
> Stanley Kubrick; directed by Stanley Kubrick

☆

MARILYN MONROE: "Water polo? Isn't that terribly dangerous?"

TONY CURTIS: "I'll say! I had two ponies drowned under me."

Some Like It Hot (1959): screenplay by Billy Wilder
and I. A. L. Diamond; director, Billy Wilder

☆

WALTER CATLETT: "I have a very pleasant surprise for you."

CHARLES LAUGHTON: "How long will you be gone?"

It Started with Eve (1941): screenplay by
Norman Krasna and Leo Townsend;
directed by Henry Koster.

☆

I only wear my diamonds just to aggravate my friends.

ZSA ZSA GABOR, actress

☆

The length of a film should be directly related to the endurance of the human bladder.

ALFRED HITCHCOCK, director

☆

Gone With the Wind is going to be the biggest flop in Hollywood history. I'm glad it'll be Clark Gable who's falling flat on his face and not Gary Cooper.

GARY COOPER, actor (and unsuccessful psychic)

☆

I got what I have now through knowing the right time to tell terrible people when to go to hell.

LESLIE CARON, dancer, actress

☆

IRENE DUNNE: "You're all confused, aren't you?"
CARY GRANT: "Uh-huh. Aren't you?"
IRENE DUNNE: "No."
CARY GRANT: "Well, you should be, because you're wrong about things being different because they're not the same. Things are different, except in a different way. You're still the same, only I've been a fool. Well, I'm not now. So as long as I'm different, don't you think things could be the same again? Only a little different?

The Awful Truth (1937): screenplay by
Vina Delmar; directed by Leo McCarey

☆

[The doctor] told me I had a dual personality. Then he lays an eighty-two dollar bill on me, so I give him forty-one bucks and say, "Get the other forty-one bucks from the other guy."

JERRY LEWIS in *The Nutty Professor* (1963):
written and directed by Jerry Lewis

Mae West

(The Era of Her Ways)

In the minds of millions, Mae West stood for Hollywood wit. Truth is, she stood for just about anything, as long as it was sexy and funny—words she considered interchangeable.

May West was so agreeable that if she had been French her name would have been Mae Oui.

She was saucy, insinuating, suggestive, but never "dirty." She dealt in a kind of ribald puritanism. She spoke with a saunter. She ambulated with hauteur. She was a mistress of the double and single entendre. Although many ventured to emulate her swiveled inflections, there was only one Mae West, and there can never be another, because America has passed the era of her ways.

When we hear that Mae West said such and so in a film,

we can be pretty sure that she had something to do with writing it. Mae was one of the very few stars who wrote most of her own stuff. She composed her successful plays for Broadway, and wrote a good many of the lines she tossed off in the movies.

She filled a long life: born in 1892, died in 1980 at age eighty-eight. What a merry message to leave behind: A lusty libido may lead to longevity.

Mae was no copycat; she invented her singular persona, which gave her parlance double meanings. Her "come up and see me sometime" became a national catch phrase (although she did not say it in quite that way).

She took nuthin' from nobody. In her first movie, the 1932 *Night After Night,* she worked with Alison Skipworth, a large woman noted for character roles. Miss Skipworth blew up when she thought Mae was stealing their scene. "I'll have you know I'm an actress," she fumed.

Mae replied, "It's all right, dearie; I'll keep your secret."

For that debut movie, Mae wrote a scene in which a hat-check girl admires Mae's shimmering appearance: "Goodness, what beautiful diamonds."

"Goodness had nothing to do with it, dearie," Mae replies, and she was on her way to stardom. (She used the line for the title of her autobiography in 1959.)

When she was on top, audiences found her irresistible. Hand on hip, toss of head, Mae could drawl outré replies to almost anything. "Are you in town for good?" Sam McDaniel asked her in *Belle of the Nineties* (1934). "I expect to be here, but not for good," Mae replied.

She made pedestrian words walk her way: "It isn't what I

say, but how I say it. It isn't what I do, but how I do it. And how I look when I do it and say it."

Mae delighted in twisting familiar expressions into sex-pressions: "It's not the men in my life, it's the life in my men that counts."

☆

When I'm good I'm very good, but when I'm bad I'm better.

☆

Whenever I'm caught between two evils, I take the one I've never tried.

☆

Is that a gun in your pocket, or are you just glad to see me?

☆

"A hard man is good to find," which was about as far as she could go on screen in her hey-hey day, but perhaps the most explicit line she ever gave her character came much later, in the 1970 movie calamity called *Myra Breckinridge*. Introduced to a rangey cowboy-type who tells her he's six-foot-seven-inches, she flaunts her hips and murmurs, "Let's forget the six feet, and talk about the seven inches."

A Galaxy of Other Remarks Mae Committed

I'm the girl who lost her reputation and never missed it.

☆

The best way to hold a man is in your arms.

☆

I never loved another person the way I loved myself.

☆

Marriage is a great institution, but I'm not ready for an institution, yet.

☆

It ain't no sin if you crack a few laws now and then, just so long as you don't break any.

☆

He who hesitates is a damned fool.

☆

To err is human, but it feels divine.

☆

I used to be Snow White, but I drifted.

☆

Too much of a good thing can be wonderful.

☆

HE: "I wonder what kind of woman you are?"
SHE: "Too bad I don't give out samples."

> **JOSEPH CALLEIA AND MAE WEST**
> in *My Little Chickadee* (1940):
> directed by Edward Cline

☆

I like to know what I'm doing.

> Explaining the mirror over her bed

☆

Beulah, peel me a grape.

> **MAE WEST,** in *I'm No Angel* (1933)

☆

Asked by the gossip columnist Hedda Hopper how she knew so much about men: "Baby, I went to night school."

☆

I've been things and seen places.

> **MAE WEST** in *I'm No Angel* (1933): screenplay by
> Lowell Brentano, Harlan Thompson, Mae West;
> directed by Wesley Ruggles

☆

GERTRUDE MICHAEL: "I don't suppose you believe in marriage."

MAE WEST: "Only as a last resort."

> *I'm No Angel* (1933): screenplay by Lowell
> Brentano, Harlan Thompson, Mae West;
> directed by Wesley Ruggles

☆

Sex must be in the face, not the body. If you have to show your body, then you haven't got it, dear.

☆

Once an effusive fan gushed up to her: "I've heard so much about you!" Mae cocked her head and said, "Yeah, but you can't prove a thing."

Hollywood's Life Is the Spice of *VARIETY*®

The exuberant show business newspaper *Variety* has added more neologisms to the American language than has any other single (or in this case, singular) publication.

Variety is the receptacle of record for the world of movies, television, recordings, radio, cabaret, home video, concerts, and the stage. It reports why Who is going where to do what to Whom, and whether any of it is, was, or will be worth doing or going.

Opinions *Variety* has got. News *Variety* has got. Get up and go *Variety* has got. Which is why each weekday morning the doers and don'ters of show business (or their designated readers) grab the paper to see what's a hit, what's a flop, who made money, who lost money, who's down, what's up, who merged, who's submerged? *Variety* is a font (Times New Roman) of news, speculation, rumor, gossip, and opinion—from figment to fact. Its financial figures, salary stats, and box office take set the industry standard.

Variety's use of inside lingo has been absorbed into the American language. Its readers are familiar with *sitcom* (television comedy), *baloney* (nonsense), *scram* or *ankle* (to leave or quit), *chopsocky* (martial arts movies), *hick* (rustic person), *payoff* (financial success), *smash* or *socko* or *boffo* (a big hit), *flop* (failure), *oater* (Western), *nabes* (neighborhood theaters), *inked* (signed), *ozoner* (drive-in theater), *sudser* (soap opera) *whodunit* (mystery), *pushover* (an easy mark), and *showbiz*.

It was in the dizzy 1920s that *Variety* first became famous for its shortcut slang and shorthand headlines. When the stock market crashed in 1929, the paper ran its now classic banner:

WALL ST. LAYS AN EGG

When rural audiences shunned movies with rustic plots, *Variety* proclaimed:

STIX NIX HICK PIX

Imagine if *Variety* had been published in early times:

MOSES ANKLES EGYPT
XERXES FLOPS IN GREECE
HANNIBAL OVER THE HILL

Variety was founded as a weekly in 1905 in New York City by Simon (Sime) Silverman. In 1933, offices were opened in Los Angeles, and from there *Daily Variety* was launched. Its most famous editors since Sime have been Abel Green, who ruled for forty years, from 1933 until 1973, and Peter Bart, who took command in 1989.

Wit and humor have infused *Variety* for almost, or more than, a century (it depends when you read this book). Its style, news coverage, savvy editors, reporters, and writers have kept *Variety* riding high as the boffo bible of showbiz.

Oscar Levant: More Than a Smattering of Wit, Music, Movies, and Pills

"There is a thin line between genius and insanity," Oscar Levant once said. "I have erased that line."

Levant's divergent careers were unparalleled. He was one of the very quickest, most erudite astringent wits of the American twentieth century. At his musical peak in the 1930s, he was America's highest paid concert pianist, renowned for his performances of the music of his idol, George Gershwin. ("Tell me, George, if you had it to do all over again, would you fall in love with yourself?")

Levant composed nineteen film scores. He appeared in thirteen movies, often as a replica of himself, frequently writing his own lines. Among his costars were Fred Astaire,

Ginger Rogers, Lauren Bacall, Bing Crosby, Joan Crawford, Doris Day, and Gene Kelly.

He was the author of three best-selling books, starting with *A Smattering of Ignorance* in 1940, all merrily (sometimes not so merrily) spearing many of America's iconiest icons.

From 1938 to 1943, Levant's wit and prodigious memory made him a national star on radio's foremost quiz program, *Information, Please.*

He was irrepressible. He chain smoked. He traveled the world. It was normal for him to drink thirty-six cups of coffee a day. He became America's best-known neurotic while spilling all over the press and airwaves details of his medical problems, drug addictions, compulsive pill swallowing, drug withdrawals, hospitalizations, and his psychiatric care.

Again and again he telephoned friends, pleading for more and more pills. "I'm contriving new means of sleeping all day," he said.

Sometimes he ended phone calls with, "I'll have to hang up now or I'll be too sleepy to take my sleeping pill."

He had born in Pittsburgh two days after Christmas in 1906, and sped most of his life in New York and Los Angeles—a whirl of music and film and famous friends and personal chaos. In 1972, at age sixty-five, Oscar Levant was killed when his heart attacked him in his California home.

♪

JACK PAAR, TV INTERVIEWER: "What did you want to be when you were a kid, Oscar?"

OSCAR LEVANT: "An orphan."

♫

I'm controversial. My friends either dislike me or hate me.

♫

The worst thing about having a mistress is those two dinners you have to eat.

♫

When Harpo Marx in California telegraphed Levant in New York with an invitation to visit, Levant wired back that he couldn't afford the train fare. Harpo offered to pay half. Levant replied, "**OKAY Stop. I'LL GO TO KANSAS CITY Stop.**"

♫

Levant arrived for his World War II physical. A psychiatrist asked, "Do you think you can kill?"

"I don't know about strangers," Levant replied, "but friends, yes."

He was deferred from military service.

♫

Levant had scimitar opinions about the celebrated American conductor and composer, Leonard Bernstein, who was at the time a fair-haired boy of music in the concert hall, on Broadway, and as a classical music guide on television.

"Leonard Bernstein [on television] has been disclosing musical secrets that have been well known for over four hundred years."

♫

"I like Lenny Bernstein," Levant said, "but not as much as he does."

♫

Bernstein uses music as an accompaniment to his conducting.

♫

Levant was leery of the young Bernstein: "I met Leonard Bernstein eighteen years ago, and I remember thinking then, 'Here is a young man who bears watching. Close watching.'"

♫

I can stand anything but failure.

As Adam Cook in *An American in Paris*

♫

On Zsa Zsa Gabor: "Zsa Zsa has learned the secret of perpetual middle age."

♫

On the actress who played goody-goody roles: "I knew Doris Day before she became a virgin."

♫

On John Wayne: "He's too subtle for me."

♫

Of his own appearance: "It's not a pretty face, I grant you. But underneath this flabby exterior is an enormous lack of character."

♫

Certain people act on me like an emetic. Phyllis Diller, the so-called comedienne, for example. I treasure every moment that I do not see her.

♫

Richard Burton can charm the pants off everyone. Especially Elizabeth Taylor.   To whom Burton was married

♫

I was an irritant to everybody. I was a catalyst when no one had asked for one.

♫

PHILIP YORDAN: "Do you want to hear about my failures?"
OSCAR LEVANT: "No, your successes are depressing enough."

♫

It's not what you are but what you don't become that hurts.   **OSCAR LEVANT,** as Sid Jeffers in *Humoresque*: screenplay by Zachary Gold and Clifford Odets; directed by Jean Negulesco

♫

Vernon Duke talks with a monocle in his throat.

♫

About a weekly TV program: "*The Jerry Lewis Show* has all the suspense of a Hitchcock thriller—the suspense of wondering when the first laugh will come."

♫

My favorite exercises are groveling, brooding, and mulling.

♫

A "woman's movie" is one where the woman commits adultery all through the picture and at the end her husband begs her to forgive him.

Y'Don't Say—II

I'll bet your father spent the first years of your life throwing rocks at the stork.

GROUCHO MARX to Chico Marx in *At the Circus* (1939): screenplay by Irvin Brecher; directed by Edward Buzzell

We were young, gay, reckless! The night I drank champagne from your slippers—two quarts. It would have held more, but you were wearing innersoles.

> **GROUCHO,** romancing Margaret Dumont in *At the Circus*: screenplay by Irving Brecher; directed by Edward Buzzell

☆

GROUCHO MARX: "Martha dear, there are many bonds that will hold us together through eternity."

MARGARET DUMONT: "Really, Wolf? What are they?"

GROUCHO MARX: "Your government bonds, your savings bonds, your liberty bonds . . ."   *The Big Store*

☆

You've got to remember that these are just simple farmers. They're people of the land. The common clay of the New West. You know—morons.

> **GENE WILDER** to Cleavon Little in *Blazing Saddles*: screenplay by Mel Brooks, Andrew Bergman, Richard Pryor, Norman Steinberg, Alan Uger; story by Andrew Bergman

☆

Sure, forgive your enemies, but first get even.

> **JAMES CAGNEY** as Nick Condon in *Blood on the Sun*: screenplay by Lester Cole; directed by Frank Lloyd

☆

In fact, civilization and syphilization have advanced together.   **ANTHONY HOPKINS** in *Bram Stoker's Dracula* (1992): screenplay by James V. Hart; directed by Francis Ford Coppola

☆

I have the same goal I've had ever since I was a girl. I want to rule the world.   **MADONNA** singer, actress

☆

I believe in large families; every woman should have at least three husbands.   **ZSA ZSA GABOR,** actress

☆

I did this picture. I did that picture. I went skiing. Then I did another picture. Then I went swimming. And I was happily married. Who gives a damn?

CLAUDETTE COLBERT, actress

☆

My father warned me about men and booze, but never mentioned a word about women and cocaine.

TALLULAH BANKHEAD, actress

☆

Never mind what I tell you to do—do what I tell you.

W. C. FIELDS in *The Big Broadcast of 1938*: screenplay by Walter DeLeon, Francis Martin, Ken Englund; directed by Mitchell Leisen

☆

Don't do it the way I did it. Do it the way I meant it.

OTTO PREMINGER, directing Cornell Wilde and Linda Darnell on the set of *Forever Amber* (1941)

☆

If I had my life to live again, I'd make the same mistakes, only sooner. **TALLULAH BANKHEAD,** actress

☆

I only put clothes on so that I'm not naked when I go out shopping. **JULIA ROBERTS,** actress

☆

When you act with your clothes on, it's a performance. When you act with your clothes off, it's a documentary. I don't do documentaries. **JULIA ROBERTS,** actress

☆

A nonentity can be just as famous as anybody else if enough people know about him.

GRACIE ALLEN, comedienne

☆

When I'm old, I'm never going to say, "I didn't do this," or "I regret that." I'm going to say, "I don't regret a damn thing. I came, I went, and I did it all."

KIM BASINGER, actress

☆

If you rest, you rust. **HELEN HAYES,** actress

☆

It's not easy to get the weight off. I've been walking, jogging three miles a day. But you know what the best way is? Young men. **ARETHA FRANKLIN,** singer

☆

I tell my conservative women friends who bother me about my youthful lover to "fuck off" or go get them one of their own. **URSULA ANDRESS,** actress

☆

God is love, but get it in writing.

GYPSY ROSE LEE, famous ecdysiast

☆

Christians can have big tits, too.

JANE RUSSELL (bountifully bosomed
passionate religionist)

☆

Why do we all have to be naked to get along?

JULIA ROBERTS, actress

☆

If you have never been hated by your child, you have
never been a parent.   **BETTE DAVIS,** actress

☆

Have you tried curiosity?

DOROTHY PARKER, writer
to a friend who had to kill her cat

☆

Boredom is a great motivator.

UMA THURMAN, actress

☆

I don't want to star opposite an unknown Swedish broad.

GEORGE RAFT, who turned down the Humphrey
Bogart role opposite Ingrid Bergman in
Casablanca (1942)

☆

A dog teaches a boy fidelity, perseverance, and to turn around three times before lying down.

ROBERT BENCHLEY, humorist, writer, actor

☆

A good detective can't sleep because a piece of the puzzle is missing, and a bad cop can't sleep because he has a guilty conscience.

AL PACINO in *Insomnia* (2002): written by Hillary Seitz; directed by Christopher Nolan

☆

If you didn't know how old you were, how old would you be? **DAVID BROWN,** producer

☆

Shirley MacLaine: "This place is crawling with celebrities. I'm the only person here I never heard of."

Sweet Charity (1969): screenplay by Peter Stone; directed by Bob Fosse

☆

David Niven told a lot of great Hollywood stories in interviews and in his books. One of my favorites was about Loretta Young: "When she was young, Loretta Young was pretty. It was her looks, not her talent that got her cast in film after film. Cecil B. DeMille told me the story of directing her in *The Crusades.* She was doing a scene urging

Richard the Lion-Hearted to fight. Loretta read the line: "Richard, you gotta save Christianity!" Not very convincing. So DeMille took Loretta aside and asked her to put some awe into her line reading. They reshot the scene, and she said: "Aw, Richard, you gotta save Christianity!"

☆

Acting is the most minor of gifts and not a very high-class way to earn a living. After all, Shirley Temple could do it at the age of four.   **KATHARINE HEPBURN,** actress

☆

Put me in the last fifteen minutes of a picture and I don't care what happened before. I don't even care if I was in the rest of the damn thing—I'll take those fifteen minutes.

BARBARA STANWYCK, actress, in an interview

☆

RALPH BELLAMY: "He's got a lot of charm."
ROSALIND RUSSELL: "He comes by it naturally. His father was a snake."

His Girl Friday (1940): screenplay by
Charles Lederer; directed by Howard
Hawks

☆

"Dear Mr Wallis: Just read *Sea Wolf.* You told me in your office that it would be a 50–50 part. I am sorry to say it is just the opposite."   **GEORGE RAFT,** actor, in telegram
to Hal Wallis, producer

☆

RYAN O'NEAL: "What are you doing? This is a one-way street."

BARBRA STREISAND: "I'm only going one way."

> *What's Up, Doc?* (1972): screenplay by Buck Henry, David Newman, Robert Benton; directed by Peter Bogdanovich

☆

BURT REYNOLDS, briefly retired from acting in the late 1970s: You can only hold your stomach in for so many years.

☆

How is Tall, Dark, and Obnoxious?

> **MARJORIE DAVIES** to John Wayne in *They Were Expendable* (1945): screenplay by Frank Wead; directed by John Ford

☆

I think that the most important thing a woman can have—next to talent, of course—is her hairdresser."

> **JOAN CRAWFORD,** actress

☆

No, I'm breaking it in for a friend.

> **GROUCHO MARX,** actor, comedian, when asked if Groucho was his real name

☆

I had the radio on.

> **MARILYN MONROE,** actress, asked if she really had
> nothing on in the [calendar] nude photograph

☆

Last week, I went to Philadephia, but it was closed.

> **W. C. FIELDS,** unique comic actor, writer, juggler

☆

A rich man is nothing but a poor man with money.

> **W. C. FIELDS,** unique comic actor, writer, juggler

☆

Nobody can be exactly like me. Sometimes I even have
trouble doing it. **TALLULAH BANKHEAD,** actress

☆

Autograph hunting is the most unattractive manifesta-
tion of sex-starved curiosity. **SIR LAURENCE OLIVIER,** actor

☆

Acting is merely the art of keeping a large group of people from coughing. **SIR RALPH RICHARDSON,** actor

☆

Hedy Lamarr once complained to her cameraman that he
wasn't shooting her as beautifully as he'd done ten years
before, on another picture. He had to be tactful, he wanted

to keep his job, so he informed her, "I'm sorry, but you must remember that I was ten years younger then. . . ."

BILLY WILDER, director

☆

Gary Cooper and Greta Garbo are the same person. After all, have you ever seen them in a movie together?

ERNST LUBITSCH, director

☆

Raquel Welch—a moron with less on.

TOTIE FIELDS, entertainer

☆

Honey, that Totie Fields is one well-fed white woman. When that gal sits around the house, she sits around the house!

MOMS MABLEY, comedienne

☆

The stupidest question I've ever been asked is whether Hermione Gingold is my real name. Now I just say, "Not really. I was born Norma Jean Baker. . . ."

HERMIONE GINGOLD, actress

☆

A comedian is not a man who says funny things. A comedian is one who says things funny.

ED WYNN, comedian

☆

One more drink and I'd have been under the host.

DOROTHY PARKER, writer

☆

Horse sense is good judgment, which keeps horses from betting on people.

W. C. FIELDS, unique comic actor, writer, juggler

☆

GAMBLER: "Say, is this a game of chance?"
CUTHBERT J. TWILLIE: "Not the way I play it."

W. C. FIELDS (as Twillie) in *My Little Chickadee* (1940)

☆

You can tell a lot about a fellow's character by his way of eating jellybeans.

RONALD REAGAN, actor, governor, president

☆

A merry Christmas to all my friends except two.

W. C. FIELDS, unique comic actor, writer, juggler

☆

GROUCHO MARX: "It's all right. That's in every contract. That's why they call it a sanity clause."
CHICO MARX: "You can't fool me. There ain't no Sanity Claus."

A Night at the Opera (1935): screenplay by George S. Kaufman and Morrie Ryskind; directed by Sam Wood

☆

I wanted to be the first woman to burn her bra, but it would have taken the fire department four days to put it out.

DOLLY PARTON, large-bosomed singer and actress

☆

"Sneak preview: A place where four or five men, making four or five thousand a week, go to watch a pimply faced kid write *It stinks* on a card." **NUNNALLY JOHNSON,** writer

☆

Forget it, Looey. No Civil War picture ever made a nickel. **IRVING THALBERG,** producer, to Louis B. Mayer regarding film rights to *Gone With the Wind*

☆

Movies are a fad. Audiences really want to see live actors on a stage. **CHARLIE CHAPLIN,** actor, writer, composer

George S. Kaufman
(The Great Collaborator)

When George S. (for Simon) Kaufman was born on November 16, 1889, first he cried, then went on to gurgle, crawl, walk, run, talk, and write, so that by 1914 he was doing a column for the *Washington Times.*

He progressed to the *Tribune* and the *Times,* both in New York, and became a sought-after reviewer and essayist, a writer of Hollywood comedies, and a playwright who, as coauthor, twice won the Pulitzer Prize.

He had a swift and cutting wit. His writing was satiric, often sardonic, almost always funny, and in public his expression was dour, although some (unidentified) were said to have seen Kaufman smile.

His precept was never "I'd rather do it myself." He was a

born collaborator. His most famous works were *The Royal Family* and *Stage Door,* both written with Edna Ferber; *Of Thee I Sing* and *Let 'em Eat Cake,* both with Morrie Ryskind; and *Once in a Lifetime, You Can't Take It with You, The Man Who Came to Dinner,* and *George Washington Slept Here,* all with Moss Hart.

★

While working in Hollywood, an incompetent writer was fired by the studio. A couple of weeks later, Kaufman encountered the man in the hall. "Ah, I see you're still here," said Kaufman. "Forgotten but not gone."

★

Bridge was his favorite game, maybe because it is played in collaboration with a partner. But Kaufman, a master player, was vexed by ineptitude. I assume that if his bridge partner was stupid, Kaufman would bid adieu.

★

A sheepish bungling partner asked him how *he* would have played the hand. "Under an assumed name," said Kaufman.

★

Another partner, whose bidding was unfathomable, asked permission to go to the men's room. "Sure," said Kaufman. "It'll be the first time today I'll know what you've got in your hand."

★

Kaufman, a man shy about his person, was easily embarrassed. Knowing this, his frequent producer, Jed Harris, called for a meeting, and when Kaufman arrived he found Harris sitting totally nude, and he remained nude throughout the conference. Finally, as Kaufman was leaving at the door, he turned to Harris and said, "Jed, your fly is open."

★

Who can forget Charles Laughton as the sadistic Captain Bligh in *Mutiny on the Bounty*? Or as Quasimodo, the misshapen bell ringer in the cathedral of Notre Dame. Speaking one day of Bligh, Laughton told Kaufman he was meant for the *Bounty* role because he came from a seafaring family. To which Kaufman said, "Then no doubt you also come from a long line of hunchbacks?"

★

When Kaufman discovered that a producer in a rural summer theater was not paying him royalties, the debtor pleaded that his was just a small insignificant theater.

"Then you'll go to a small, insignificant jail," Kaufman said.

★

Kaufman was asked how he would do it if he wanted to kill himself: "With kindness," the great man said.

The Sweet Bye and Bye

Death and humor often hang out together; they even occasionally embrace. Funny tombstones aplenty attest to the lighter side of afterlife. The devil is often shown rocking with laughter, but I have never seen an image of God laughing, not even a smile. Mark Twain wrote, "There is no humor in heaven." Only in hell is there the promise of a hot time. The British essayist Sir Max Beerbohm (1872–1956) reminded us that there is no record of anyone ever having died of laughter, and yet there are those (I hope) who will say, after rollicking in these pages, "I nearly died laughing." Movies have made merry with death (see especially *Here Comes Mr. Jordan,* 1941). No writer-actor has provided more pleasure with humor about death than has Woody Allen, but many others have also found grave humor funny.

I'm not afraid of death. I just don't want to be there when it happens.   **WOODY ALLEN** writer, director, actor

Either he's dead or my watch has stopped.

> **GROUCHO MARX,** taking a pulse
> in 1937's *A Day at the Races*

My uncle is a southern planter. He's an undertaker in Alabama.   **FRED ALLEN,** comedian, actor

Blonds make the best victims. They're like virgin snow that shows up the bloody footprints.

> **DIRECTOR NUNNALLY JOHNSON'S** theory
> of killing movie characters

The chief problem about death is the fear that there may be no afterlife. That's a depressing thought, particularly for those who have bothered to shave.   **WOODY ALLEN**

He's too nervous to kill himself. He wears his seatbelt in a drive-in movie.

> *The Odd Couple* (1968): Walter Matthau scoffing
> at Jack Lemmon committing suicide

Death is the greatest kick of all. That's why they save it for last. **RON SILVER** in *Blue Steel* (1990)

If your mother were alive, she'd turn over in her grave!

> **ANTHONY QUINN** to John Turturro
> in Spike Lee's *Jungle Fever* (1991)

I do not believe in an afterlife, although I am bringing a change of underwear. **WOODY ALLEN**

They shoot too many pictures and not enough actors.

> **COLUMNIST WALTER WINCHELL**

If I could drop dead right now, I'd be the happiest man alive! **SAM GOLDWYN,** during a studio crisis

I don't want to achieve immortality through my work, I want to achieve it through not dying. **WOODY ALLEN**

Michael Curtiz

(A Director Beyond Words)

If there were any sort of movie that Michael Curtiz (*ker-TEEZ*) couldn't direct, I don't know what it could be, with perhaps one exception: He couldn't direct a truly bad movie.

From the romantic *Casablanca* to *The Adventures of Robin Hood,* from the musical *Yankee Doodle Dandy* to the dramatic *Mildred Pierce,* he could do it all.

Curtiz is one of my most favorite directors, perhaps because I never had to work for him. Those who did often bridled under his serrated spur. He was demanding, he was unreasonable, yet some who complained loudest often gave their best performances when he was at the helm—even though for them his set was a helm on earth.

After shooting *Night and Day,* its star, Cary Grant, confronted him: "If I'm ever stupid enough to be caught working with you again, you'll know that I'm either broke or I've lost my mind."

James Cagney, who won an Academy Award in 1942 for his singing-and-dancing portrayal in Curtiz's *Yankee Doodle Dandy,* said, "The only thing Curtiz has to say is 'Don't do it the way I showed you, do it the way I mean.'"

What would Warner Bros. have done without Curtiz? He made more than one hundred movies for Warner, and he brought his films in on time and on budget. Throughout the 1930s and '40s his pictures were the epitome of "That Warner Touch" (or, more likely, "That Warner Punch-Smack-Caress-Smash").

Curtiz was born Mihali Kertesz in Hungary on Christmas Eve, 1888, and died in America in 1962, age seventy-four. Arriving in the 1920s, he learned to pronounce individual English words, but he was baffled when putting them together. The fractured results amused his friends and colleagues, and over his office door there hung a sign:

CURTIZ SPOKEN HERE.

Accepting the Academy Award for Casablanca: "So many times I have a speech ready but no dice. Always a bridesmaid, never a mother."

☆

Directing two stars in a romantic scene: "Could you get a little closer apart?"

☆

On a musical: "It's dull from beginning to end. But it's loaded with entertainment."

☆

To Gary Cooper, on horseback: "Now ride off in all directions."

☆

To a child star: "By the time I was your age, I was fifteen!"

☆

Complaining to an assistant: "Everyone wants to jump into my throat."

☆

A gofer, sent on an errand, returned with the wrong stuff, exasperating Curtiz: "The next time I send a dumb sonofabitch to do something, I go myself!"

☆

On a set design for a movie: "I want this house overfurnished in perfect taste."

☆

Bring on the empty horses.

While directing *The Charge of the Light Brigade* in 1936

☆

This man Cole Porter, he sticked to purpose of making good music, come hell or hayride.

> Expressing admiration for the composer Cole Porter,
> the subject of *Night and Day*

☆

Greeted with, "Howdy, stranger," Curtiz said, "What do you mean 'stranger'? I don't even know you."

☆

Complaining to Bette Davis about a scene: "There's a fling in the ointment."

☆

Picking up the phone: "I'm out, but call me back in an hour."

Booray for Hollywood

Many cities have been zapped for fun. "Greater Cleveland" is an oxymoron. "I went to Philadelphia, but it was closed." "New York is a nice place to visit, but I wouldn't want to live there." In the 1930s and '40s, "Brooklyn" ignited laughter, and Mel Blanc's railroad announcer intoning, "Anaheim, Azusa, and Cucamonga!" always brought down the house on Jack Benny's comedy radio show. But no city surpasses Hollywood (and by extension Southern California), as a target of ridicule.

☆

Hollywood is like being nowhere and talking to nobody about nothing. **MICHELANGELO ANTONIONI,** director

☆

Strip away the phony tinsel of Hollywood and you'll find the real tinsel underneath.

OSCAR LEVANT, concert pianist, actor, writer, wit

☆

I don't want to live in a city where the only cultural advantage is that you can make a right turn on a red light.

WOODY ALLEN in *Annie Hall* (1977):
written and directed by Woody Allen

☆

All creative people should be required to leave California for at least three months every year.

GLORIA SWANSON, actress

☆

In Hollywood, the women are all peaches. It makes one long for an apple occasionally. **SOMERSET MAUGHAM,** writer

☆

You can take all the sincerity in Hollywood, place it in the navel of a fruit fly, and still have room enough left for three caraway seeds and a producer's heart.

FRED ALLEN, writer, humorist

☆

California: The west coast of Iowa.

JOAN DIDION, writer

☆

Hollywood—that's where they give awards to Charlton Heston for acting.

SHIRLEY KNIGHT, actress

☆

I believe that God felt sorry for actors so he created Hollywood to give them a place in the sun and a swimming pool. The price they had to pay was to surrender their talent.

SIR CEDRIC HARDWICKE in his autobiography, *A Victorian in Orbit*

☆

Seventy-two suburbs in search of a city.

DOROTHY PARKER, writer

☆

A dreary industrial town controlled by hoodlums of enormous wealth, the ethical sense of a pack of jackals, and taste so degraded that it befouled everything it touched.

S. J. PERELMAN, writer

☆

The only "ism" Hollywood really believes in is plagiarism.

DOROTHY PARKER, writer

☆

There were times when I drove along the Sunset Strip and looked at those buildings or when I watched the fashionable film colony arriving at some premiere . . . that I fully expected God in his wrath to obliterate the whole she-bang.   **S. J. PERELMAN,** writer

☆

Hollywood didn't kill Marilyn Monroe, it's the Marilyn Monroes who are killing Hollywood.

BILLY WILDER, director, writer

☆

No one has a closest friend in Hollywood.

SHEILAH GRAHAM, writer, columnist

☆

In Hollywood, you can get sued for telling the truth. After all, it's Hollywood where the truth lies.

ANTHONY PERKINS, actor

☆

Hollywood is a sewer with service from the Ritz Carlton.

WILSON MIZNER, Hollywood wit,

writer, gambler, actor

☆

Hollywood is a great place to live—if you happen to be an orange.   **FRED ALLEN** (also said of California)

☆

The way to be successful in Hollywood is to be as obnoxious as the next guy.   **SYLVESTER STALLONE,** actor

☆

Hollywood: Ten million dollars' worth of intricate and highly ingenious machinery, functioning elaborately to put skin on baloney.   **GEORGE JEAN NATHAN,** writer, critic

☆

I wouldn't live in California. All that sun makes you sterile.   **ALAN ALDA,** actor

☆

It's a scientific fact that if you stay in California, you lose one point of IQ every year.   **TRUMAN CAPOTE,** writer

Harry Cohn

(but some there were who liked him)

Of the legendary movie moguls, Harry Cohn alone was marked a loud, crude tyrant. Frequently admired for what he accomplished, frequently despised for the way he accomplished it.

By a significant many he was loathed. To them his nickname was Genghis Cohn. A bitter antagonist, the Hollywood columnist Hedda Hopper, sniped: "You had to stand in line to hate him."

Yet, when his heart failed, and he died in February 1958, his funeral overflowed with the multitudes who arrived for his service. Red Skelton had an explanation for the crowd: "It only proves what they always say—give the public what they want, and they'll come out for it."

A number of the famous who knew him well (including Frank Sinatra, Danny Kaye, and Jack Lemmon) testified that a good-hearted man lived inside that ogre suit. Bob Thomas wrote in his biography *King Cohn* that he "took an odd pride in his reputation for ruthlessness." So proud that he did good deeds surreptitiously lest he be discovered and thought tenderhearted and soft.

Harry Cohn was born in New York in 1891. As a young man, fascinated by show business, he is said to have formed a one-room movie company on Broadway with $250 in launch money. In 1924, he organized in Hollywood as Columbia, and by the end of the decade he had built it into a major studio where $250 was pin money.

Columbia didn't have the clout of MGM or Warner Bros., but Cohn's relentless drive, his instinct for the public's taste, his reliance on good writers and directors (most especially Frank Capra), and his unshakable self-confidence, combined to create some of Hollywood's most celebrated films. Among them: *It Happened One Night, Mr. Deeds Goes to Town, Lost Horizon. Mr. Smith Goes to Washington, The Jolson Story, From Here to Eternity,* and *On the Waterfront.*

Columbia pictures won some forty-five Oscars, quite a record for a man who was forever self-conscious about his lack of education and scorned by most of the industry.

☆

Like Goldwyn, Cohn admired good writers. He would take jibes and tolerate a lot of guff from favored writers that he wouldn't stand for from anyone else. Once he complained to the writer Jo Swerling that Swerling's wife had driven into Cohn's Rolls-Royce in the Columbia parking lot. "She must have thought you were in it," Swerling said.

☆

At lunch in the executive dining room, Cohn asked, "Where do you think I was last night?"

"Night school?" said Norman Krasna, a writer.

☆

During a staff meeting, Cohn proclaimed, "I'm going to England next week."

Krasna called out, "Gee, Mr. Cohn, can I go along with you?"

Cohn stared at him. "Go with me!" he snorted. "Now why the hell would I take a punk like you to England with me?"

"As interpreter?"

☆

According to Bob Thomas's *King Cohn,* one morning the mogul ordered a group of employees to his office and waved a script at them.

"I pay you bastards thousands of dollars a week to know something and what do I get? Ignorance! Tell me," he said condescendingly to a producer. "When is this picture supposed to take place?"

"I'd say about 1200 A.D."

"Well, I never went to college like you sons of bitches, but I can tell you one thing: people didn't say 'yes, siree' in 1200. Goddammit, all through the script you've got 'em saying, 'Yes, siree.'"

"Could I see where you mean, Harry?" a writer asked.

"Right here!" Cohn thrust the script across the desk, banging his finger on a passage. The writer read it and said, "But Harry, that's 'Yes, sire'!"

☆

Cohn was proud of his ability to pick new actresses. Of one who caught his eye, he said, "She has talent and personality. Give me two years and I'll make her an overnight star."

☆

A day came when Judy Holliday auditioned for Cohn, also known as "the move-making mogul on many a madchen," or "lech." Judy, forewarned, squelched his very first advance: She reached inside her blouse, pulled out her falsies, and said, "Here's what you're looking for."

☆

Lucille Ball was set to be a star in Cecil B. DeMille's *The Greatest Show on Earth* when she discovered she was pregnant. She and her agent and her husband, Desi Arnaz, went to give DeMille the bad news. She said, "Mr. DeMille, I'm going to have a baby."

"Well, do something about it," said DeMille.

"But Desi and I have been hoping for this for ten years."

DeMille shrugged and wished them well. As they were leaving, DeMille took Arnaz aside. "Congratulations," he said, "you're the only man in history who screwed Lucille Ball, Columbia Pictures, Paramount Pictures, Cecil B. DeMille, and Harry Cohn, all at the same time."

S * X

Hollywood's Favorite 3-Letter Word

DIANE KEATON: "It's hard to believe you haven't had sex for two hundred years."

WOODY ALLEN: "Two hundred and four if you count my marriage."

> In *Sleeper* (1973): screenplay by Woody Allen, and Marshall Brickman; directed by Woody Allen.

☆

I've tried several varieties of sex. The conventional position makes me claustrophobic. And the others give me either a stiff neck or lockjaw.

TALLULAH BANKHEAD, actress

☆

Sex appeal is fifty percent what you've got and fifty percent what people think you've got.   **SOPHIA LOREN,** actress

☆

I have a steak at home. Why should I go out for a hamburger?   **PAUL NEWMAN,** actor, director, on his enduring marriage to Joanne Woodward, actress

☆

I think nudity on screen is disgusting, shameful, and unpatriotic. But if I were twenty-two, with a great body, it would be artistic, tasteful, patriotic, and a progressive, religious experience.   **SHELLEY WINTERS,** actress

☆

Gilbert Roland was a wonderful husband. In one room of the house.   **CONSTANCE BENNETT,** his former wife

☆

Today, you see girls doing on the screen what they used to do off the screen to get on screen.   **GENE AUTRY,** actor

☆

The only difference between sex and death is, with death you can do it alone and nobody's going to make fun of you.

WOODY ALLEN

☆

The most unlikely women are the most explosive lovers.

DAVID BROWN, author, *Brown's Guide to Growing Gray*

☆

Nunnally Johnson, the late and great Hollywood writer, once cabled a friend who had sailed off on a honeymoon with a bride thirty years younger, "You'll be all right—but don't show off." **DAVID BROWN,** producer

☆

Perform sex? I don't think I'm up for a performance, but I'll rehearse with you if you'd like.

WOODY ALLEN in *Sleeper* (1973): screenplay by Woody Allen and Marshall Brickman; directed by Woody Allen

☆

If I'd had as many love affairs as I've been given credit for, I'd be in a jar at the Harvard Medical School.

FRANK SINATRA, singer, actor

☆

The important thing in acting is to be able to laugh and cry. If I have to cry, I think about my sex life. If I have to laugh, I think about my sex life.

GLENDA JACKSON, actress

☆

I'm a virgin. I'm just not very good at it.

> **GLENDA JACKSON** in *Hot Shots!* (1991): screenplay by Pat Proft and Jim Abrahams; directed by Jim Abrahams.

☆

I've never watched anybody make love, so how do you know if you're doing it right?

> **KEVIN COSTNER,** actor, in an interview

☆

If Clark had an inch less, he'd be called the Queen of Hollywood.

> **CAROLE LOMBARD,** third wife of Clark Gable, nicknamed "The King of Hollywood"

☆

JILL ST. JOHN: "I'll finish dressing."
SEAN CONNERY: "Oh, please don't. Not on my account."

> *Diamonds Are Forever* (1971): screenplay by Richard Maibaum and Tom Mankiewicz; directed by Guy Hamilton

☆

I act from my crotch. That's where my force is. Sexuality is my strongest driving force and as I get older and older, I find it is less and less, shall we say, compelling.

> **JEREMY IRONS,** actor

☆

I like older men. They're so grateful.

> **GRETA GARBO** in *Two-Faced Woman* (1941): screenplay by S. N. Behrman, Salka Viertel, George Oppenheimer; directed by George Cukor

☆

I've got everything Betty Grable has—only I've had it longer.

> **DAME MAY WHITTY,** famous as an old lady spy in *The Lady Vanishes* (1938), on her physical appearance

☆

Listen, I appreciate this whole seduction thing you've got going, but let me give you a tip. I'm a sure thing."

> **JULIA ROBERTS** to Richard Gere in *Pretty Woman* (1990): screenplay by J. F. Lawton, directed by Gary Marshall

☆

Rumor had it that the sex-obsessed Clara Bow laid everything but the linoleum.

> **ANONYMOUS**

☆

He wasn't a satisfying lover. I often tried to distract him from the bedroom.

> **JOAN CRAWFORD,** actress and Clark Gables's mistress for many years

☆

God knows I love Clark, but he's the worst lay in town.

> **CAROLE LOMBARD,** actress and Gable's third wife

☆

I guess I'll just have to practice more.

CLARK GABLE, actor

☆

Glamour is just sex that got civilized.

DOROTHY LAMOUR, actress

☆

There but for a typographical error go I.

DOROTHY PARKER, watching
party guests ducking for apples

☆

A man is only as old as the woman he feels.

GROUCHO MARX, actor, comedian

☆

I think vibrators are great. They keep you out of stupid
sex.   **ANN HECHE,** actress

☆

My understanding of women goes only as far as the pleasures.   **MICHAEL CAINE,** actor

☆

Rhonda Fleming to Robert Mitchum: "You always go around leaving your fingerprints on a girl's shoulder?"

> *Out of the Past* (1947): screenplay by Geoffrey
> Homes; directed by Jacques Tourneur

☆

I saw losing my virginity as a career move.

> **MADONNA,** singer, actress

If you have a vagina and a point of view, that's a deadly combination. **SHARON STONE,** actress

☆

I'm a practicing heterosexual . . . but bisexuality immediately doubles your chances for a date on Saturday night.

> **WOODY ALLEN**

☆

When grown-ups do it it's kind of dirty—that's because there's no one to punish them. **TUESDAY WELD,** actress

☆

I had now made about forty-five pictures, but what had I become? I knew all too well: a phallic symbol. All over the world I was, as a name and personality, equated with sex.

> **ERROL FLYNN,** actor, *My Wicked, Wicked Ways*
> (New York: Putnam, 1959)

☆

That was the most fun I ever had without laughing.

WOODY ALLEN referring to sex in *Annie Hall*
(1977): screenplay by Woody Allen and
Marshall Brickman

☆

I'll come and make love to you at five o'clock. If I'm late,
start without me. **TALLULAH BANKHEAD,** actress

☆

My dad told me, "Anything worth having is worth waiting for." I waited until I was fifteen.

ZSA ZSA GABOR, actress

Men vs. Women vs. Men

WILFRED HYDE-WHITE: "Are you a man of good character where women are concerned?"

REX HARRISON: "Have you ever met a man of good character where women are concerned?"

> *My Fair Lady* (1964): screenplay by Alan J. Lerner;
> directed by George Cukor

JEAN HARLOW: "Would you be good enough to shut the door?"
ROBERT TAYLOR: "It's already shut."
JEAN HARLOW: "On your way out."

> *Personal Property* (1937): screenplay by Hugh Mills
> and Ernest Vajda; directed by W. S. Van Dyke

I find that girl completely resistible.

> **OSCAR LEVANT** in *The Barkleys of Broadway*
> (1949): screenplay by Betty Comden,
> directed by Charles Walters

STERLING HAYDEN: "How many men have you forgotten?"
JOAN CRAWFORD: "As many women as you've remem-
bered."   **JOHNNY GUITAR** (1954): screenplay by Philip
> Yordan; directed by Nicholas Ray

Getting married has ruined a lot of good men.

> **TEX BAIRD** In *Dodge City* (1939): screenplay by
> Robert Bruckner; directed by Michael Curtiz

Tell me, Mrs. Wright, does your husband interfere with
your marriage?

> **OSCAR LEVANT TO JOAN CRAWFORD** in *Humoresque*
> (1944): screenplay by Clifford Odets and Zachary
> Gold; directed by Jean Negulesco

I found out Carole Lombard wasn't a natural blonde.
We're in her dressing room, talking. She starts undressing. I
didn't know what to do. She's talking away and mixing per-

oxide and some other liquid in a bowl. With a piece of cotton she begins to apply the liquid to dye the hair around her honeypot. She glanced up, and saw my amazed look, and smiled. "Relax, Georgie, I'm just making my collar and cuffs match." **GEORGE RAFT,** actor

PAUL NEWMAN TO PATRICIA NEAL: "The only question I ever ask a woman is, 'What time is your husband coming home?'" *Hud* (1963): screenplay by Irving Ravetch and Harriet Frank; directed by Martin Ritt

MARLON BRANDO: "No matter who you get married to, you wake up married to somebody else."

Guys and Dolls (1955): written and directed by Joseph L. Mankiewicz

SHELLEY WINTERS IN AN INTERVIEW: "In Hollywood all marriages are happy. It's trying to live together afterward that causes the problems."

BETTE DAVIS: "Bill's thirty-two. He looks thirty-two. He looked it five years ago. He'll look it twenty years from now. I hate men."

All About Eve (1950): written and directed by Joseph L. Mankiewicz

LOUIS JOURDAN: "The only people who make love all the time are liars."

> *Gigi* (1958): screenplay by Alan Jay Lerner; directed by Vincente Minnelli

PETER O'TOOLE TO KATHARINE HEPBURN: "Well, what shall we hang, the holly or each other?"

> *The Lion in Winter* (1968): screenplay by James Goldman; directed by Anthony Harvey

If a man wants to get it right, he's looked up to and respected. If a woman wants to get it right, she's difficult and impossible. If he acts, produces, and directs, he's called multitalented. If she does the same thing, she's called vain and egotistical." **BARBARA STREISAND,** singer, actress

A woman doing comedy doesn't offend me, but sets me back a bit. I, as a viewer, have trouble with it. I think of her as a producing machine that brings babies in the world.

> **JERRY LEWIS,** on Lucille Ball and comediennes in general

Husbands are like fires. They go out when unattended.

> **ZSA ZSA GABOR,** actress

Remember, *I'm* the leading lady.

> **JULIE ANDREWS,** actress, to Rock Hudson, actor,
> during filming of *Darling Lili* (1970)

You're not too smart, are you? I like that in a man.

> **KATHLEEN TURNER,** actress to William Hurt, actor,
> in *Body Heat*

The more I see of men, the more I like dogs.

> **CLARA BOW,** actress

Strong women leave big hickeys.

> **MADONNA,** singer, actress

Always a bride, never a bridesmaid.

> **OSCAR LEVANT,** concert pianist, actor, writer, wit
> about Elizabeth Taylor's many marriages

A man in love is incomplete until he has married. Then he's finished.   **ZSA ZSA GABOR,** actress

You see a girl a couple of times a week and sooner or later she thinks you'll divorce your wife. Not fair, is it?

> **FRED MACMURRAY** to Jack Lemmon
> in *The Apartment*

When Fernando [Lamas] proposed to me, he said, "Let me take you away from all this." And I said, "Away from all what? I'm a movie star!"   **ESTHER WILLIAMS,** actress

I did not want to be known as Kate Smith.

> **KATHARINE HEPBURN,** replying to why
> she divorced Ludlow Ogden Smith

I begged Richard [Dawson] not to go to the States. You know what happens to most British actors who go there . . . they finish up playing butlers or opening fish-and-chips stands. With Dickie, it was worse: He became host of something called *Family Feud*.   **DIANA DORS,** actress

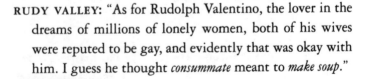

RUDY VALLEY: "As for Rudolph Valentino, the lover in the dreams of millions of lonely women, both of his wives were reputed to be gay, and evidently that was okay with him. I guess he thought *consummate* meant to *make soup*."

My fourth husband and I had tremendous fights. He used his fists more than his mouth. They ought to rewrite the ceremony: "In sickness and in hell . . ." **BETTE DAVIS** actress

Noel [Coward] and I were in Paris once. Adjoining rooms, of course. One night, I felt mischievous, so I knocked on Noel's door, and he asked, "Who is it?" I lowered my voice and said, "Hotel detective. Have you got a gentleman in your room?" He answered, "Just a minute, I'll ask him."

BEATRICE LILLIE, actress

Do you know what it means to come home at night to a woman who'll give you a little love, a little affection, a little tenderness? It means you're in the wrong house.

GEORGE BURNS comedian, actor

One evening when Leo Rosten was at Groucho Marx's home for dinner, as Leo was leaving he paused at the door and said, "I'd like to say good-bye to your wife."

"Who wouldn't?" Groucho said.

You mean apart from my own?

ZSA ZSA GABOR, actress, when asked
how many husbands she had had

I've only slept with the men I've been married to. How many women can make that claim?

ELIZABETH TAYLOR, actress

Listen, the love between two men is beautiful. I'd love to be between, say, Tyrone Power and Montgomery Clift. Hell, I was born in the wrong gender! **NANCY WALKER,** actress

Lily Tomlin has been in and out of the closet more times than my hunting jacket. **ROCK HUDSON,** actor

Why does a woman work ten years to change a man's habits and then complain that he's not that man she married? **BARBRA STREISAND,** singer, actress

Every minute this broad spends outside my bed is a waste of time. **MICHAEL TODD** (1907–52), regarding his wife, actress Elizabeth Taylor

I can play a heterosexual. I know how they walk. I know how they talk. You don't have to be one to play one.

LILY TOMLIN, comic actress, on playing it straight

GARY COOPER: "I can tell you what an Indian will do to you, but not a woman."

> *The Plainsman* (1936): screenplay by Courtney Ryley Cooper and Harold Lamb; directed by Cecil B. DeMille

WILLIAM HOLDEN, IN REFERENCE TO GRACE KELLY'S CHARACTER: "All wives start out as Juliets and end up as Lady Macbeths."

> *The Country Girl* (1954): written and directed by George Seaton

GRACE KELLY, OFFERING PICNIC CHICKEN TO CARY GRANT: "Do you want a leg or a breast?"

> *To Catch a Thief* (1955): screenplay by John Michael Hayes; directed by Alfred Hitchcock

An outmoded silly convention started by the caveman and encouraged by the florists and jewelers.

> **OLIVIA DE HAVILLAND** on marriage in *The Strawberry Blonde* (1941): screenplay by Julius J. Epstein and Philip C. Epstein; directed by Raoul Walsh

GINGER ROGERS'S OPINION OF GENE RAYMOND: "I'll bet he's broken both his legs running after two women at the same time." *Flying Down to Rio* (1933): screenplay by Cyril Hume, H. W. Hanemann, Erwin Gelsey; directed by Thornton Freeland

Tallulah Bankhead, the famous deep-throated actress, visited the ladies' powder room at New York's fashionable Plaza Hotel. When she realized there was no toilet paper in her stall, and noticing a handbag on the floor next to hers, she called out, "Do you have any toilet paper in there?"

The woman looked and said, "Oh, gosh, no."

A pause, then Tallulah's low voice boomed out: "You got two tens for a twenty?"

> *"Oh, Wad Some Power the Giftie Gie Us/To See Oursels as Ithers See Us!"*
>
> **ROBERT BURNS,** 1786

I look like a duck.   **MICHELLE PFEIFFER,** actress

In some situations I was difficult, in odd moments impossible, in rare moments loathsome, but at my best, unapproachably great.

OSCAR LEVANT, concert pianist, actor, writer, wit

When I'm really hot, I can walk into a room and if a man doesn't look at me, he's probably gay.

KATHLEEN TURNER, actress

♪

I am just too much.   **BETTE DAVIS,** actress

♪

When I'm good I'm very good, but when I'm bad I'm better.   **MAE WEST,** actress

♪

My life is composed of random, tangential disparate episodes. Five wives: many liaisons, some more memorable than the marriages. The hunting. The betting. The Thoroughbreds. Painting, collecting, boxing. Writing, directing, and acting . . .   **JOHN HUSTON,** actor

♪

Honestly, I think I've stretched a talent, which is so thin it's almost transparent, over quite an unbelievable term of years.   **BING CROSBY,** singer, actor

♪

Pictures make me look like a twelve-year-old boy who flunked his body-building course.   **JULIE HARRIS,** actress

♪

Everything you see I owe to spaghetti.

SOPHIA LOREN, actress

♪

I rather like my reputation, actually, that of a spoiled genius from the Welsh gutter, a drunk, a womanizer; it's rather an attractive image. **RICHARD BURTON,** actor

♪

I have my standards. They may be low, but I have them.

BETTE MIDLER, actress

♪

I never said I wanted to be alone. I said I wanted to be left alone. There is a difference. **GRETA GARBO,** actress

♪

I had pretty much always been promiscuous, but right after I started *Cheers,* well, I was going on about three dates a day. As a guy, you're raised to get as much as you can. Sex, sex, sex, that's what you're after. But after a while, I realized what I was doing was foolhardy. Still, it took some time to travel from the brain groinward.

WOODY HARRELSON, actor

♪

I know I've been a perfect bitch. But I couldn't help myself. **BETTE DAVIS,** actress

♪

When I look at myself, I am so beautiful, I scream with joy. **MARIA MONTEZ,** actress

♫

I'm magnificent. I'm five feet eleven inches, and I weigh 135 pounds, and I look like a race horse.

JULIE NEWMAR, actress

♫

I look fabulous for my age.   **JANE FONDA,** actress

♫

My butt! It fascinates me . . . I like it so much that when I dance, I'm always looking back at it.

TORI SPELLING, actress

♫

I'm a ballbuster, blonde or brunette.

ASHLEY JUDD, actress

♫

I am simple, complex, generous, selfish, unattractive, beautiful, lazy, and driven.

BARBARA STREISAND, singer, actress

♫

I never know how much of what I say is true.

BETTE MIDLER, actress, comedienne

♫

I'm just a clean-cut Mongolian boy.

YUL BRYNNER, actor

♫

I never go out unless I look like Joan Crawford the movie star. If you want to see the girl next door, go next door.

JOAN CRAWFORD, actress

♫

I'm fiercely intelligent.   **SHARON STONE,** actress

♫

I am a sensitive writer, actor, and director. Talking business disgusts me. If you want to talk business, call my disgusting personal manager.   **SYLVESTER STALLONE,** actor

♫

I'm a very physical person. People don't credit me with much of a brain, so why should I disillusion them?

SYLVESTER STALLONE, actor

♫

I have bursts of being a lady, but it doesn't last long.

SHELLEY WINTERS, actress

♫

I arrived in Hollywood without having my nose fixed, my teeth capped, or my name changed. That is very gratifying to me.   **BARBRA STREISAND,** singer, actress

♫

I'm so gullible. I'm so damn gullible. And I am so sick of being gullible. **LANA TURNER,** actress, seven times married

♪

I don't especially like the way I look sometimes, but I never met a man since I was fourteen that didn't want to give me an argument about it.

> **LANA TURNER** in *The Postman Always Rings Twice* (1946): screenplay by Harry Ruskin and Niven Busch; directed by Tay Garnett

♪

Everybody wants to be Cary Grant. Even I want to be Cary Grant. **CARY GRANT,** actor

♪

I improve by misquotation. **CARY GRANT,** actor

♪

People hate me because I am a multifaceted, talented, wealthy, internationally famous genius.

> **JERRY LEWIS,** actor

♪

I'm a bad woman, but I'm damn good company.

> **FANNY BRICE,** Ziegfeld Follies star

♪

The best time I ever had with Joan Crawford was when I pushed her down the stairs in *Whatever Happened to Baby Jane.*

BETTE DAVIS, actress

♪

Through it all, I have remained consistently and nauseatingly adorable. In fact, I have been known to cause diabetes.

MEG RYAN, actress

♪

I'm as pure as the driven slush.

TALLULAH BANKHEAD, actress

♪

I'm the female equivalent of a counterfeit twenty-dollar bill. Half of what you see is a pretty darn good reproduction, the rest is a fraud.

CHER, actress, singer

♪

I don't know where you'd find buttocks like mine, dear.

TRACY ULLMAN, actress, explaining why she didn't use a body double in *Ready to Wear*

♪

I'm a study of a man in chaos in search of frenzy.

OSCAR LEVANT, concert pianist, actor, writer, wit

Y'Don't Say—III

All my shows are great. Some of them are bad, but they're all great.　　　**SIR LEW GRADE,** producer

☆

How does Keanu Reeves work with Coppola and Bertolucci and I don't get a shot at that, know what I'm saying?　　　**CHARLIE SHEEN,** actor

☆

My acting range? Left eyebrow raised, right eyebrow raised.　　　**ROGER MOORE,** actor

☆

I'd hate to be a teetotaler. Imagine getting up in the morning and knowing that's as good as you're going to feel all day.　　　　　　　　**DEAN MARTIN,** singer, actor

☆

He was able to do a very emotional scene with tears in his eyes, and pinch my fanny at the same time.

SHELLEY WINTERS, actress,
about Fredric March, actor

☆

Men are those creatures with two legs and eight hands.

JAYNE MANSFIELD, actress

☆

He once told me, "I want to impregnate every woman in the world," though I didn't realize until later how literally he meant it.　　　　　**RUTH WARRICK,** actress, about
Anthony Quinn, actor

☆

I'd rather be smart than a movie star.

NATALIE PORTMAN, actress

☆

I've done an awful lot of stuff that's a monument to public patience.　　　　　　　　**TYRONE POWER,** actor

☆

Otto was one of those directors you can't listen to because he doesn't know anything at all about the process of acting. I didn't think he was ever right.

> **FAYE DUNAWAY,** actress, about
> Otto Preminger, director

☆

LA is the most isolated, competitive, nasty situation I've ever seen.

> **SARAH POLLEY,** actress

☆

It would have been cheaper to lower the Atlantic.

> **SIR LEW GRADE,** producer, discussing his
> production of *Raise the Titanic*

☆

The four-foot Pole you wouldn't want to touch with a ten-foot pole.

> **KENNETH TYNAN,** critic, about
> Roman Polanski, director

☆

The truth is, I don't want people to know me. I don't know a thing about my favorite actors. I don't think you should. Then they become personalities.

> **BRAD PITT,** actor

☆

You could put all the talent I had into your left eye and still not suffer from impaired vision.

> **VERONICA LAKE,** actress

☆

The relationship between the makeup man and the film actor is that of accomplices in crime.

MARLENE DIETRICH, actress

☆

The greatest actor that ever lived—everything you can dream of, times ten—was Charles Laughton.

BILLY WILDER, director

☆

I have the face of an aging choirboy and the build of an undernourished featherweight. If you can figure out my success on the screen you're a better man than I am.

ALAN LADD, actor

☆

With the Academy Awards, if you're standing there and looking out, you're going to see many people who can't find their butt with their hand. **SEAN PENN,** actor

☆

In movies you're a product. And if I'm a product, I'm a Tabasco sauce. I'm not a sort of shepherd's pie, and that's the way it is. **JOHN MALKOVICH,** actor

☆

Most of Hollywood's so-called women's movies are based on men's fantasies. **TAMARA DAVIS,** director

☆

For the most part, young actors in Hollywood are actors by default. They're morons.   **MATT DAMON,** actor

☆

My dentist said to me the other day, I've enough problems in my life, so why should I see your films?

DAVID GREENBERG, actor

☆

I'm afraid you'll never make it as an actor. But as a star, I think you might well hit the jackpot.

ORSON WELLES, director,
to Joseph Cotten, actor

☆

Big audiences in Britain are mind dead. The best British audience I ever played to was in Broadmoor asylum.   **BRIAN COX,** actor

☆

To Raoul Walsh, a tender love scene is burning down a whorehouse.   **JACK L. WARNER,** producer

☆

The only time he was in trouble was when he tried to act.   **FRED ZINNEMANN,** director,
about Gary Cooper, actor

☆

Even when you win the rat race, you're still a rat.

JOAN COLLINS, actress

☆

Anyone who gets a raw deal in a film studio is no more deserving of pity than someone who gets beaten up in a brothel. A gentleman has no business in either place.

SIR ALEXANDER KORDA, producer

☆

I was sitting one day and thinking about cannibalism, because that's what guys like me do . . . and I thought, suppose a guy was washed up on a rocky island, how much of himself could he eat?   **STEPHEN KING,** writer

☆

I wish I'd never been an actor! I wish I'd never had success! I'd rather have been a streetwalker, selling my body, than selling my tears and my laughter, my grief and my joy.

KLAUS KINSKI, actor

☆

The golf course is the only place I can go dressed like a pimp and fit in perfectly.   **SAMUEL L. JACKSON,** actor

☆

The great thing in life is to be very beautiful and very stupid.   **TERENCE DAVIES,** director

☆

I'm a whore, all actors are whores. We sell our bodies to the highest bidder. **WILLIAM HOLDEN,** actor

☆

A good film is when the price of the admission, the dinner, and the baby-sitter was well worth it.

SIR ALFRED HITCHCOCK, director

☆

Movies are one of the bad habits that have corrupted our century. They have slipped into the American mind more misinformation in one evening than the Dark Ages could master in a decade. **BEN HECHT,** writer

☆

To be a good director you've got to be a bastard. I'm a bastard and I know it. **HENRY HATHAWAY,** director

☆

Don't tell me. Suggest. But don't tell.

FRANK SINATRA, singer, actor

☆

You know that bank I used to cry all the way to?

LIBERACE, pianist

☆

Filmmaking is like spermatozoa: Only one in a million makes it. **CLAUDE LELOUCH,** director

☆

I have no use for humility, I am a fellow with an exceptional talent. **JACKIE GLEASON,** comedian, actor

☆

The movies are an eruption of trash that has lamed the American mind and retarded Americans from becoming cultured people. **BEN HECHT,** writer

☆

I don't use any particular method. I'm from the let's pretend school of acting. **HARRISON FORD,** actor

☆

My country is still so repressed. Our idea of what is sexual is blonde hair, long legs, twenty-two years old. It has nothing to do with humor, intelligence, warmth; everything to do with teeth and cleavage. **SALLY FIELD,** actress

☆

If I'm such a legend, why am I so lonely?

JUDY GARLAND, singer, actress

☆

I had the stage mother of all time. If I wasn't well and didn't want to go on, she'd yell "Get out on that stage or I'll tie you to the bedpost."

JUDY GARLAND, singer, actress

☆

Make 'em redecorate your office. That's primary, to let them know where you stand. Then, when you're shooting interior sequences, use your own interior decorator and set dresser. That way, everything on the set will fit your house when you're finished. **BLAKE EDWARDS,** director

☆

I've always had the ability to say to the audience, watch this if you like, and if you don't, take a hike.

CLINT EASTWOOD, actor

☆

The motion picture business is run by corporate thieves.

RICHARD DREYFUSS, actor

☆

Dere's a million good lookin' guys in the world, but I'm a novelty. **JIMMY (SCHNOZZLE) DURANTE,** actor, comedian.

☆

My theory is that no matter how many enemies you make, you can always work for *their* enemies.

ROBERT DUVALL, actor

☆

I always cry when I watch myself on screen.

CLINT EASTWOOD, actor

☆

Of course, I couldn't go out in the street in clothes like this, I'd get picked up. Come to think of it, it might be fun.

LIBERACE, pianist

☆

I love Mickey Mouse more than any woman I've ever known.

WALT DISNEY, animator

☆

I dress for women, and undress for men.

ANGIE DICKINSON, actress

☆

I've yet to be convinced that the film business is a profession for adults.

FREDERICK FORSYTH, writer

☆

I believe women should be sexual. And why not? What a great thing to be: a sexual woman, coming of age and discovering sensuality and the intoxication of it. I've seen so many movies about women who don't like sex and really don't want to have sex, or have that posey stuff in Calvin Klein ads. Well, that's just not true and I'm sick of that myth being out there. What I'd like to do is develop movies that better reflect my generation of women.

JODIE FOSTER, actress

☆

I'm actually a thin, serious person, but I play fat and funny, but only for the movies.

DOM DELUISE, actor, comedian

☆

We have no obligation to make art. We have no obligation to make a statement. To make money is our only objective. **MICHAEL EISNER,** Disney Studios, 1981

☆

God felt sorry for actors, so he gave them a place in the sun and a lot of money. All they had to sacrifice was their talent. **CLAUDE RAINS,** actor

☆

It's great to be black in Hollywood. When a black actor does something, it seems new and different just by virtue of the fact that he's black. I've got it so much easier than Brad Pitt or Tom Cruise. **WILL SMITH,** actor

☆

There's only one thing that can kill the movies, and that's education. **WILL ROGERS,** wit

☆

I'm Jewish. I don't work out. If God had intended me to bend over, he'd have put diamonds on the floor.

JOAN RIVERS, comedienne

☆

I don't want actors reasoning with me about motivation and all that bull. All I want them to do is learn the goddamn lines and don't bump into each other.

JASON ROBARDS, actor

☆

I am very shy. I am more the convent girl type. Characters in movies help you do stuff that you would never do in life—like having a gun, or being a whore.

GERALDINE PAILHAS, actress

☆

Nothing is beneath me if it pays well. I've earned the right to damn well grab whatever I can in the time I've got left.

SIR LAURENCE OLIVIER, actor

☆

The only thing you have always to remember: Never ever sleep with a man until he gives you a pure white stone of at least ten carats.

PAULETTE GODDARD, actress

☆

I don't accept flowers. I take nothing perishable.

PAULETTE GODDARD, actress

☆

Cocaine is God's way of saying you're making too much money.   **ROBIN WILLIAMS,** actor, comedian

☆

Before he can pick up an ashtray he discusses his motivation for a couple of hours. You want to tell him to pick up the ashtray and shut up.   **JEANNE MOREAU,** actress, about Burt Lancaster, actor

☆

Don't say yes until I finish talking.

DARRYL F. ZANUCK, producer

☆

I did a picture in England one winter and it was so cold I almost got married.   **SHELLEY WINTERS,** actress

☆

I started at the top and worked down.

ORSON WELLES, actor, director

☆

Gluttony is not a secret vice.

ORSON WELLES, director, actor

☆

If you have physical attractiveness you don't have to act.

RAQUEL WELCH, actress

☆

To write a script today means working for a committee of people who know nothing about movies, as opposed, say, to real estate or the higher art of bookkeeping.

GORE VIDAL, writer, 1996

☆

I'm not an old-fashioned romantic. I believe in love and marriage, but not necessarily with the same person.

JOHN TRAVOLTA, actor

☆

One day I'll make a film for the critics, when I have money to lose. **CLAUDE LELOUCH,** director

☆

Wherever Thalberg (head of production at MGM) sits, is always the head of the table. Hollywood saying, 1930s

☆

If someone is dumb enough to offer me a million dollars to make a picture, I'm certainly not dumb enough to turn it down. **ELIZABETH TAYLOR,** actress

☆

I steal from every movie ever made.

QUENTIN TARANTINO, director

☆

I've been at this so long that I knew everyone in the business long before I became famous, and I didn't value many of them. Now, suddenly, the people who were coarse and rude to me before treat me as though we've never met, and now I'm fabulous and isn't it fabulous we're chatting.

SHARON STONE, actress

☆

If I had my career over again? Maybe I'd say to myself, speed it up a little.   **JIMMY STEWART,** actor

☆

When I was about eight years old, I happened to mention to my father that I wanted to be an actress and he gave me a wallop in the face.   **GRETA SCACCHI,** actress

☆

My confidence only peaked when I was forty-nine and I said, yes, I'm gay.   **SIR IAN MCKELLEN,** actor

☆

When you're down and out, something always turns up—usually the noses of your friends.

ORSON WELLES, actor, director

☆

My kids never had the advantage I had. I was born poor.

KIRK DOUGLAS, actor

☆

I've played so many hookers they don't pay me in the regular way any more. They leave it on the dresser.

SHIRLEY MacLAINE, actress

☆

My dad was the town drunk. Usually that's not so bad, but New York City? **HENNY YOUNGMAN,** comedian

☆

I was street-smart—but unfortunately the street was Rodeo Drive. **CARRIE FISHER,** actress

☆

I was raised in the Jewish tradition, taught never to marry a gentile woman, never shave on Saturday, and, most especially, never to shave a gentile woman on Saturday.

WOODY ALLEN, writer, actor, director

☆

I drink to make other people interesting.

GEORGE JEAN NATHAN, writer, critic

☆

If you ask me to play myself, I will not know what to do. I do not know who or what I am.

PETER SELLERS, actor

☆

Generally, I don't look at scripts. At $200,000 a week, what do I care what it's about?   **MICKEY ROONEY,** actor

☆

This is a terrific script. It just needs a complete rewrite.

> **DIRECTOR PETER BOGDANOVICH** to writer Alvin
> Sargent while directing *Paper Moon* (1973)

☆

My movies were the kind they show in prisons and airplanes, because nobody can leave.   **BURT REYNOLDS,** actor

☆

Being a star has made it possible for me to get insulted in places where the average Negro could never hope to get insulted.   **SAMMY DAVIS JR.,** actor, singer, dancer

☆

A fan club is a group of people who tell an actor he is not alone in the way he feels about himself.

> **JACK CARSON,** actor

☆

He gives her class, and she gives him sex.

> **KATHARINE HEPBURN'S** opinion of
> Fred Astaire and Ginger Rogers

☆

My daddy is a movie actor, and sometimes he plays good guy and sometimes he plays the lawyer.

> **MALCOLM FORD,** explaining to preschool mates
> what his father, Harrison, does for a living

☆

Take it from me: Marriage isn't a word, it's a sentence.

> **KING VIDOR,** director

☆

I've had a wonderful evening—but this wasn't it.

> **GROUCHO MARX** to a Hollywood hostess

☆

Who made the picture, the *shark?*

> **A STEVEN SPIELBERG FRIEND,** angry that Spielberg
> was not nominated for a Best Director Oscar
> when *Jaws* was up for Best Picture

☆

The Oscar-winning music for *Jaws* was composed by the musically proliferous John Williams. That wonderful man told me of an encounter one of his idols, the composer Bernard Herrmann, had with the director Alfred Hitchcock during the filming of *Lifeboat* (1944). The entire story takes place in a lifeboat in midocean, in which a disparate group of shipwreck survivors are attempting to, well, survive. When the picture was being edited, Hitchcock turned to the composer and said, "Wait a minute, Bernie, we're in the middle of the ocean! Where is your music coming from?"

Herrmann didn't miss a beat: "The same place your cameras are coming from."

☆

The eminent producer David Brown had such an enormous success making *Jaws,* that Universal immediately ordered *Jaws 2.* Another moneymaker, and two were enough for Brown. When Sid Sheinberg, the head of Universal, wanted *Jaws 3,* Brown and his partner, Richard Zanuck, declined. Sheinberg pressed and pressed until Brown finally said he'd agree, but only if Universal would use his title.

"Which is?" asked Sheinberg.

Brown was ready: "Jaws 3, People 0."

☆

From which direction?

> **GROUCHO MARX** to a woman who told him she was "approaching forty"

☆

Oh, Jim, weren't we beautiful then?

> **AVA GARDNER,** actress, to Stewart (Jim) Granger, actor, two weeks before her 1990 death at age sixty-eight

☆

It is not enough that your friend not succeed; he must also fail.

> **DAVID BROWN,** producer

☆

The sexual preferences of certain celebrities should remain a secret among the three of them.

IRV KUPCINET, Chicago columnist

☆

Money talks—and therefore you need not speak of it. Even the fool in Shakespeare's *King Lear* counseled, "Have more than thou showest." **DAVID BROWN,** producer

☆

I have everything now I had twenty years ago—except now it's all lower.

GYPSY ROSE LEE, celebrated ecdysiast turned writer

☆

I stopped believing in Santa Claus when I was six. Mother took me to see him in a department store and he asked me for my autograph. **SHIRLEY TEMPLE,** actress

☆

I am naturally suspicious of deep thinkers in relation to motion pictures. **DARRYL F. ZANUCK,** producer

☆

If you're going to make rubbish, be the best rubbish in it. **RICHARD BURTON,** actor, on his films

☆

People have been so busy relating to how I look, it's a miracle I didn't become a self-conscious blob of protoplasm.

ROBERT REDFORD, actor

☆

Just standing around looking beautiful is so boring, really boring, so boring.   **MICHELLE PFEIFFER,** actress

☆

I got started dancing because I knew that it was one way to meet girls.   **GENE KELLY,** actor, dancer, choreographer

☆

I've taken up the Bible again somewhat in the spirit of W. C. Fields—looking for loopholes.   **DAVID NIVEN,** actor

☆

I made some mistakes in drama. I thought drama was when the actors cried. But drama is when the *audience* cries.

FRANK CAPRA, director

☆

I always brought up my children not to believe in Mother's Day gifts, and now I regret it.

LAUREN BACALL, actress

☆

Thank God, I am still an atheist.   **LUIS BUNUEL,** director

☆

She'd never admit it, but I think it's Mama.

ZSA ZSA, actress, when asked who was
the oldest of the Gabor women

☆

I got all the schooling any actress needs—that is, I learned to write well enough to sign contracts.

HERMIONE GINGOLD, actress

☆

When I hear an actress say, "You know what, I'm gonna have my face done, get my tits raised, and I'm going to get another ten years out of this business," I say, "More power to you. Go do it."   **MICHELLE PFEIFFER,** actress

☆

Method acting? Mine involves a lot of talent, a glass, and some cracked ice.   **JOHN BARRYMORE,** actor

☆

Acting is a masochistic form of exhibitionism. It is not quite the occupation of an adult.

SIR LAURENCE OLIVIER, actor

☆

Miss Hepburn runs the gamut of human emotions from A to B.   **DOROTHY PARKER,** writer, critic

☆

I shall never understand the weird process by which the body with a voice suddenly fancies itself as a mind. It's about time the piano realized it has not written the concerto.   **JOSEPH MANKIEWICZ,** writer, producer

☆

No one can really like an actor.

ALFRED HITCHCOCK, director

☆

Start every day off with a smile—and get it over with.

W. C. FIELDS, unique comic actor, writer, juggler

☆

You know you're getting old when the candles cost more than the cake.   **BOB HOPE,** comedian, actor

☆

My wife was too beautiful for words, but not for arguments.   **JOHN BARRYMORE,** actor

☆

Not only is there no God, but try getting a plumber on weekends.   **WOODY ALLEN,** writer, actor, director

☆

What I look for is whether the idea is true and entertaining. However, if I were ever forced to make the choice, I would prefer it to be entertaining."

BILLY WILDER, director, writer

☆

All the things I like to do are either illegal, immoral, or fattening. **ALEXANDER WOOLLCOTT,** critic

☆

The trouble with incest is that it gets you involved with relatives. **GEORGE S. KAUFMAN,** writer

☆

To set the record straight, it was Leo Rosten at a banquet in New York who said of W. C. Fields, "Anyone who hates children and dogs can't be all bad."

GENE SHALIT, movie reviewer

☆

When doctors and undertakers meet, they wink at each other. **W. C. FIELDS,** unique comic actor, writer, juggler

☆

It's easy to direct while acting—there's one less person to argue with. **ROMAN POLANSKI,** director

☆

My mother loved children—she would have given anything if I had been one. **GROUCHO MARX,** comedian, actor

☆

I'd rather wake up in the middle of nowhere than in any city on earth. **STEVE MCQUEEN,** actor

☆

You grow up the day you have the first real laugh at yourself.   **ETHEL BARRYMORE,** actress

☆

I've been rich and I've been poor. Rich is better.
                    SOPHIE TUCKER, The Last of the Red Hot Mamas

☆

A great many people have asked how I manage to get so much work done and still keep looking so dissipated.

                    ROBERT BENCHLEY, humorist, actor, author

☆

Anyone can do any amount of work provided it isn't the work he is supposed to be doing at that moment.

                    ROBERT BENCHLEY, humorist, actor, author

☆

If I had to give young writers advice, I'd say don't listen to writers talking about writing.   **LILLIAN HELLMAN,** writer

☆

Sometimes I think it sounds like I walked out of the room and left the typewriter running.   **GENE FOWLER,** screenwriter,
                    describing his own work

☆

After I decided to become a Jew, only then did I learn the Jews don't really have all the money. When I found out Rockefeller and Ford were *goyim*, I almost resigned.

SAMMY DAVIS JR., actor

☆

Several tons of dynamite are set off in this [John Wayne] picture—none of it under the right people.

JAMES AGEE, critic, writer

☆

I'm not against the police; I'm just afraid of them.

ALFRED HITCHCOCK, actor, director, writer

☆

It took me fifteen years to discover I had no talent for writing, but I couldn't give it up because by that time I was too famous.   **ROBERT BENCHLEY,** humorist, actor, author

☆

When I was a kid I said to my father one afternoon, "Daddy, will you take me to the zoo?" He answered, "If the zoo wants you, let them come and get you."

JERRY LEWIS, comedian, actor

☆

I find television very educating. Every time somebody turns on the set, I go into the other room and read a book.

GROUCHO MARX, comedian, actor

☆

I always keep a supply of stimulant handy in case I see a snake—which I also keep handy.

W. C. FIELDS, unique comic actor, writer, juggler

☆

If at first you don't succeed, try, try, again. Then quit. There's no use being a damn fool about it.

W. C. FIELDS, unique comic actor, writer, juggler

☆

The most important thing in acting is sincerity. If you can fake that, you've got it made.

GEORGE BURNS, comedian, actor

☆

Know your lines and don't bump into the furniture.

SPENCER TRACY's advice for young actors

☆

People often become actresses because of something they dislike about themselves: so they pretend they are someone else.

BETTE DAVIS, actress, interview

☆

I always say, keep a diary and some day it'll keep you.

MAE WEST, actress

☆

If I made Cinderella, the audience would immediately be looking for a body in the coach.

ALFRED HITCHCOCK, director

☆

I've been in Who's Who, and I know what's what, but it'll be the first time I ever made the dictionary.

MAE WEST: Letter to the RAF, 1940s, on having an inflatable lifejacket named after her

☆

I read Shakespeare and the Bible and I can shoot dice. That's what I call a liberal education.   **TALLULAH BANKHEAD,** actress

☆

Here lies W. C. Fields. I would rather be living in Philadelphia.   **W. C. FIELDS,** suggested epitaph for himself

☆

The best fame is a writer's fame: It's enough to get a table at a good restaurant, but not enough that you get interrupted when you eat.   **FRAN LEBOWITZ,** writer

☆

And my parents finally realize that I'm kidnapped and they snap into action immediately: They rent out my room.

WOODY ALLEN

☆

There are easier things in this life than being a drag queen. But I ain't got no choice. Try as I may, I just can't walk in flats.

HARVEY FIERSTEIN in his *Torch Song Trilogy* (1979)

☆

The only thing I regret about my life is the length of it. If I had to live my life again I'd make all the same mistakes only sooner.   **TALLULAH BANKHEAD,** actress

☆

He taught me housekeeping: When I divorce I keep the house.   **ZSA ZSA GABOR,** actress,

grateful to her fifth husband

☆

I am married to a fine actor named Rip Torn. . . . The mail carriers are used to our mailbox, which reads Torn Page.   **GERALDINE PAGE,** actress

☆

Somebody left the cork out of my lunch.

W. C. FIELDS, unique comic actor, writer, juggler

☆

Poor Princess Grace and poor Princess Diana. Every girl's waiting for her prince to come, but why do they always have to look like Prince Rainier or Prince Charles?

CAROL CHANNING, actress

☆

To work as hard as I've worked at anything and then have some yo-yo come up and say, "Take off those dark glasses and let's have a look at those blue eyes" is really discouraging.

PAUL NEWMAN, actor, director

☆

One of my chief regrets during my years in the theater is that I couldn't sit in the audience and watch me.

JOHN BARRYMORE, actor

☆

Rudy Vallee tried to have Beverly Hills change the name of his street to *Rue de Vallee,* but he was voted down.

☆

In Italy for thirty years under the Borgias they had warfare, terror, murder, and bloodshed, but they produced Michelangelo, Leonardo Da Vinci, and the Renaissance. In Switzerland, they had brotherly love, they had five hundred years of democracy and peace, and what did they produce? The cuckoo clock.

ORSON WELLES in *The Third Man* (1949):
screenplay by Graham Greene and
Alexander Korda; directed by Carol Reed

☆

Of the Marx Brothers [S. J. Perelman] once said, "I did two films with them, which in its way is perhaps my greatest distinction in life, because anybody who ever worked on any picture for the Marx Brothers said he would rather be chained to a galley oar and lashed at ten-minute intervals than ever work for these sons-of-bitches again."

> *S. J. Perelman—A Life,* by Dorothy Hermann

☆

One morning I shot an elephant in my pajamas. How he got in my pajamas I don't know.

> **GROUCHO MARX** on his days in Africa in *Animal Crackers* (1930): screenplay by Morrie Ryskind and George S. Kaufman; directed by Victor Heerman

☆

MARY LAROCHE: "What does your husband do?"
MAUREEN STAPLETON: "I don't know, he's dead."

> *Bye Bye Birdie* (1963): screenplay by Irving Brecher, Michael Stewart, Charles Strouse, Lee Adams; directed by George Sidney

☆

When shooting *Prince and the Showgirl,* I said to Marilyn [Monroe], "Why can't you get here on time, for fuck's sake?" And she replied, "Oh, do you have that word in England, too?"

> **SIR LAURENCE OLIVIER,** actor

☆

John Huston treats me like an idiot—"Honey, this" and "Honey, that."

> **MARILYN MONROE,** actress

☆

They used to shoot Shirley Temple through gauze. You should shoot me through linoleum.

TALLULAH BANKHEAD, actress

☆

Now I can wear high heels again.

NICOLE KIDMAN after her divorce from the diminutive Tom Cruise

☆

I am the foe of moderation, the champion of excess.

TALLULAH BANKHEAD, actress

☆

NYDIA WESTMAN: "Don't big empty houses scare you?"
BOB HOPE: "Not me, I used to be in vaudeville."

The Cat and the Canary (1939): screenplay by Walter De Leon, Lynn Starling, John Willard; directed by Radley Metzger

☆

Damn you, I'm not an actor, I'm a movie star!

PETER O'TOOLE in *My Favorite Year* (1982): screenplay by Norman Steinberg and Dennis Palumbo; directed by Richard Benjamin

☆

In my movie *Querelle,* Brad Davis plays a sailor. He wears pants so tight that you know what religion he isn't.

RAINER WERNER FASSBINDER, director

☆

I gonna tell you something. *Bonanza* is not an accurate depiction of the West. . . . You ever see the show? It's a fifty-year-old father with three forty-seven-year-old sons. You know why they get along so well? They're all the same age.

JACKIE GAYLE in *Tin Men* (1987): screenplay by
Barry Levinson; directed by Barry Levinson

☆

That dreadful picture [*The Producers*]. I can't bear to watch it, even on a small television. I'm rather sorry I did it. I must have needed the money. Living in Hollywood weakens one's motives.

ESTELLE WINWOOD, actress

☆

I was in Hitchcock's *Lifeboat.* So was Tallulah Bankhead, who didn't wear panties, and each morning when we climbed into a lifeboat—up on a mechanical rocker—she gave the cast and crew a hell of a view, hiking up her skirt! Eventually someone complained to Hitch, who didn't want to get involved. He explained that it was an interdepartmental matter—involving wardrobe, costume, and possibly hairdressing. . . .

HUME CRONYN, actor

☆

Menahem Golan should stick to producing. Money, not art, is his favorite subject. Every time he directs, it's the Golan Depths. **ALDO RAY,** actor

☆

He's new, but he knows more than he lets on . . . a refreshing change from the usual directors who know less than they pretend. **JOAN CRAWFORD** on Steven Spielberg

☆

When I directed Dame Edith Evans, she asked me, "I don't look seventy, do I? Now be honest." I replied, "No, love, you don't. Not anymore."

TONY RICHARDSON, director

☆

I always felt sorry for Herbert Marshall because of his wooden leg. Of course, we never mentioned it. One day he and I were chatting, and I saw the columnist Sheilah Graham heading our way. I told him without thinking, "Oh, Bart, watch out for her. She'll talk your leg off."

JOAN FONTAINE, actress

☆

Today's actors are more handsome; the actresses are not. . . . Then Herbert Marshall was a star, even a romantic symbol, although he had lost a leg in the First [World] War. There was a famous story that he was once the houseguest of a famous hostess, and he tripped in her house and seemed to be in pain. So she rushed to her husband and asked him whether she should call a doctor or a carpenter?

MARLENE DIETRICH, actress

☆

I did a movie with Duke [John] Wayne and was very surprised to find out he had small feet, wore lifts, and a corset. Hollywood is seldom what it seems. . . .

ROCK HUDSON, actor

☆

John Wayne had four-inch lifts in his shoes. He had the overheads on his boat accommodated to fit him. He had a special roof put in his station wagon. . . . The son of a bitch, they probably buried him in his goddamn lifts.

ROBERT MITCHUM, actor

☆

We used to have actresses trying to be stars; now we have stars trying to be actresses. **SIR LAURENCE OLIVIER,** actor

☆

I deny that I ever said actors are cattle; what I said was that actors should be treated like cattle.

ALFRED HITCHCOCK, director

☆

In Hollywood, a starlet is the name for any woman under thirty who is not actively employed in a brothel.

BEN HECHT, screenwriter in the 1930s

☆

Irving Thalberg, the producing powerhouse at MGM in the 1930s, was so frequently late for appointments in his own office, it was rumored that he did not know how to tell time and was unable to read a calendar. Not only hours, but *days* late was not unusual for him. His habit of keeping people waiting in his outer office forever (+ −) was legendary. Dorothy Parker, the screenwriter and celebrated wit, arrived for a meeting, lost patience when the sun set, and left town to continue an affair with an out-of-town lover. She subsequently received a stern letter from Thalberg demanding an explanation for her absence from the script meeting.

Dorothy Parker's reply to *Dear Mr. Thalberg* concluded: "I can only offer the explanation that I was too fucking busy, and vice versa."

☆

When the actress Helen Hayes was invited to Hollywood, the moguls were perplexed by her plain appearance. Louis B. Mayer, lord of all he ruled at MGM, called her in: "An actress must have sex appeal. I've decided to give you this dress to see what it will do for you."

Ms. Hayes looked over the slinky white satin gown and said, "That isn't a dress—that's an invitation."

☆

During the 1930s heydays of the big Hollywood studios, a power of the Hollywood press was the Hearst columnist Louella Parsons. She could be cruel, she was relentless, and she could make or break careers. Sam Goldwyn lamented, "Louella is stronger than Samson. He needed two columns to bring down the house. Louella can do it with one."

☆

A fellow actor who had made a picture with Ginger Rogers told me, "She's not very easy to know, is she?"

I said, "Not if you're lucky, old man."

CARY GRANT, actor

☆

Czar of all the rushes.

B. P. SCHULBERG, president of Paramount Pictures, describing Louis B. Mayer, Poo Bah of MGM

☆

Put my ashes in a box and tell the messenger to bring them to Louis B. Mayer's office with a farewell message from me. Then, when the messenger gets to Louis's desk, I want him to open the box and blow the ashes in the bastard's face.

B. P. SCHULBERG'S last request to his son, Budd, author of the classic Hollywood novel, *What Makes Sammy Run?*

☆

I played an unsympathetic part—myself.

OSCAR LEVANT on his role in *Humoresque* (1946)

☆

To be a success an actress must have the face of Venus, the brain of Minerva, the grace of Terpsichore, the memory of Macaulay, the figure of Juno, and the hide of a rhinoceros.

ETHEL BARRYMORE, actress

☆

What does "inept" mean?

JAYNE MANSFIELD on reading the reviews of her stage debut in *Will Success Spoil Rock Hunter*

☆

When I saw my first film test, I ran from the projection room screaming. **BETTE DAVIS,** actress

☆

I play John Wayne in every part regardless of the character, and I've been doing okay, haven't I?

JOHN WAYNE, actor

☆

Why do actors think they're so goddamn important? They're not. Acting is not an important job in the scheme of things. Plumbing is. **SPENCER TRACY,** actor

☆

I think Spencer always thought that acting was a rather silly way for a man to make a living.

KATHARINE HEPBURN, actress, on Spencer Tracy, actor

☆

Invested with great words or with the majesty of a noble thought, the actor is often confused with the source of power. Once deprived of that which makes him seem magnificent, he is deflated like an empty windbag.

JOSEF VON STERNBERG, director

☆

After *The Wizard of Oz* I was typecast as a lion, and there aren't all that many parts for lions. **BERT LAHR,** actor

☆

Whatever success I've had is a lot of instinct and a little luck. I just go by how I feel. **CLINT EASTWOOD,** actor

☆

It sure beats working. **ROBERT MITCHUM** on acting

☆

Do I subscribe to the Olivier school of acting? Ah, nuts! I'm an actor. I just do what comes naturally.

HUMPHREY BOGART, actor

☆

I don't know which makes me vomit worse—the horned toads from the cloak-and-suit trade, the shanty Irish, or the gentlemen who talk of Screen Art.

STEPHEN VINCENT BENET, writer, poet

☆

John Ford isn't exactly a bum, is he? Yet he never gave me any manure about art. He just made movies and that's what I do.   **JOHN WAYNE,** actor

☆

When I first saw von Stroheim at the wardrobe tests for his role as Rommel (in *Five Graves to Cairo*), I clicked my heels and said: "Isn't it ridiculous, little me directing you? You were always ten years ahead of your time." And he replied, "Twenty."   **BILLY WILDER,** director

☆

Anyone can direct a good picture if he's got a good script.
GARSON KANIN, writer

☆

Where do the noses go?

> **INGRID BERGMAN** to Gary Cooper as she prepares
> for her first kiss in *For Whom the Bell Tolls*
> (1943): screenplay by Dudley Nichols; directed
> by Sam Wood

☆

You make just one good picture and nobody will ever remember the other guy.

> **ANONYMOUS** studio executive advising Elia Kazan
> to change his name to Cezanne

☆

If you get your head above the mob, they try to knock it off. If you stay down, you last forever.

ALLAN DWAN, director

☆

Never take top billing. You'll last longer that way.

BING CROSBY, singer, actor

☆

They ruin your stories. They massacre your ideas. They prostitute your art. They trample on your pride. And what do you get for it? A fortune. **ANONYMOUS** screenwriter

☆

The basic art of motion pictures is the screenplay; it is fundamental, without it there is nothing.

RAYMOND CHANDLER, writer

☆

You call this a script? Give me a couple of $5,000-a-week writers and I'll write it myself. **JOE PASTERNAK,** producer

☆

Being a good writer is no feather bed. Writing is almost as lonely a craft as flagpole sitting (and is becoming almost as passé). You write behind a closed door, and fun is your enemy. **BEN HECHT,** writer (and one of the best and fastest)

☆

Let me tell you about writing for films. You finish your book. Now, you know where the California state line is? Well, you drive right up to that line, take your manuscript, and pitch it across. No, on second thought, don't pitch it across. First, let them toss the money over. *Then* you throw it over, pick up the money, and get the hell out of there.

ERNEST HEMINGWAY, writer

☆

There's too much pretentious nonsense talked about the artistic problems of making pictures. I've never had a goddam artistic problem in my life, never, and I've worked with the best of them. **JOHN WAYNE,** actor

☆

He got a reputation as a great actor just by thinking hard about the next line. **KING VIDOR,** director, about Gary Cooper, actor

☆

There were three things that Chico was always on—a phone, a horse, or a broad.

GROUCHO MARX, comedian, actor

☆

This [motion picture] industry must have toward that sacred thing, the mind of the child, toward that clean virgin thing, the unmarked slate, the same responsibility, the same care about the impressions made upon it, that the best clergyman or the most inspired teacher of youth would have.   **WILL HAYS,** Hollywood "censor"

☆

Will Hays is my shepherd, I shall not want. He maketh me to lie down in clean postures.

GENE FOWLER, lampooning the Hays Office code

☆

They are doing things on the screen now that I wouldn't do in bed. If I could.   **BOB HOPE,** comedian, actor

☆

The trouble with censors is they worry if a girl has cleavage. They ought to worry if she hasn't any.

MARILYN MONROE, actress, who had

☆

I think the picture stinks.

OSCAR LEVANT when asked by Darryl Zanuck
of 20th Century-Fox for an opinion about a
new Fox film.

Who the hell are you to think the picture stinks?

DARRYL ZANUCK

Who the hell do you have to be to think the picture stinks?   **OSCAR LEVANT**

If it were mine, I'd cut it up and sell it for mandolin picks. **ARTHUR CAESAR** to Darryl Zanuck after a private screening of one of his latest productions

The picture was so bad they had to do retakes before they could put it on the shelf. **KING VIDOR,** director

Cocoanuts introduced me to the Marx Brothers. *Cocoanuts* was a comedy; the Marx Brothers are comics; meeting them was a tragedy. **GEORGE S. KAUFMAN,** writer

I have no advice to give to young actors. To young, struggling actresses my advice is to keep struggling. If you struggle long enough, you will never get into trouble and if you never get into trouble, you will never be much of an actress.

GROUCHO MARX, comedian, actor

Location shooting is the Rite of Spring for certain members of the crew, who may even be happily married, and for young cast members who have never been away from home before. Holiday Inns across America are probably host to more sprung beds and screaming orgasms when a movie company comes to town than at any other time.

STEVEN SPIELBERG, director

☆

There were times when my pants were so thin I could sit on a dime and know if it was heads or tails.

SPENCER TRACY, actor

☆

Unable Obtain Bidet. Suggest handstand in shower.

BILLY WILDER visiting Paris, in a telegram to his
wife who had asked him to buy her a bidet

☆

I have God, and when you get to know Him, you find He's a livin' doll.

JANE RUSSELL, actress

☆

She thinks she doesn't get old. She told me once it was her cameraman who was getting older. She wanted me to fire him.

JOE PASTERNAK, producer,
on Doris Day, actress

☆

When I die, be sure the services are in the morning, so my friends can get to the track and not lose any time they need for betting.

ARTHUR CAESAR, actor

☆

I was in love with a beautiful blonde once; she drove me to drink. It's the one thing I'm indebted to her for.

W. C. FIELDS, unique comic actor, writer, juggler

☆

The surest sign of depression in the industry is not the cutting-down of stars' salaries or the dropping of contract players or the reductions of work crews. The surest sign is when a major studio begins laying off the relatives.

IRVIN S. COBB, humorist

☆

If all the serious lyric poets, composers, painters, and sculptors were forced by law to stop their activities, a rather small fraction of the general public would become aware of the fact and a still smaller fraction would seriously regret it. If the same thing were to happen with the movies, the social consequences would be catastrophic.

ERWIN PANOFSKY, art historian

☆

I'll tell you about those men (the producers). They were monsters and pirates and bastards right down to the bottom of their feet, but they loved *movies*. They loved *making* movies, they loved *seeing* movies, and they protected the people who worked for them. Some of the jerks running the business now don't even have faces.

RICHARD BROOKS, director, 1970

☆

When the actor and television wit Dick Cavett was a young man just starting out, he applied for a writing job on *The Jack Paar Show.* Paar said, "If you really want to make it on my show, there is something you have to do for me. Tonight, Jayne Mansfield is going to be on for the twelfth time and I don't know how to introduce her. Now, if you have any ideas, that'll be your passport to writing for my show."

Cavett did and was hired. He suggested this introduction for Hollywood's excessively voluptuous Miss Mansfield:

"And now, here they are, Jayne Mansfield."

> **DAVID BROWN,** producer and writer
> in his memoir, *Let Me Entertain You*

☆

When an actress known for her stevedore vocabulary complained that "The acoustics are terrible," Ethel Barrymore replied, "Now you can be obscene but not heard."

☆

"There's a man outside with a big black moustache."
"Tell him I've got one."

> **CHICO MARX AND GROUCHO MARX** in *Horsefeathers*
> (1932): Screenplay by Kalmar and Harry Ruby,
> S. J. Perelman, Will B. Johnstone; directed by
> Norman Z. McLeod

☆

It was a toss-up whether I'd go in for diamonds or sing in the choir. The choir lost.

> **MAE WEST** in *She Done Him Wrong* (1933):
> screenplay by Harvey F. Thew and
> John Bright; directed by Lowell Sherman

☆

"These dice ain't got no spots on 'em. They're blank."

"I had the spots removed for luck, but I remember where the spots formerly were."

> **FRANK SINATRA AND B. S. PULLY** in *Guys and Dolls* (1955): screenplay and directed by Joseph L. Mankiewicz

☆

"Would you like to buy a raffle ticket for the church for fifty cents?"

"Now what would I do with a church if I won one?"

> **LITTLE BOY AND JACKIE GLEASON** in *Papa's Delicate Condition* (1963): screenplay by Jack Rose; directed by George Marshall

☆

You still have your hourglass figure, my dear, but most of the sand has gone to the bottom.

> **BOB HOPE** in *The Lemon Drop Kid* (1950): screenplay by Frank Tashlin, Edmund Hartmann, Robert O'Brien; directed by Sidney Lanfield

☆

SHE: "Is it true that my dear, dear daddy is dead?"

HE: "I hope so. They buried him."

> **ROSINA LAWRENCE AND STAN LAUREL** in *Way Out West* (1937): screenplay by Jack Jevne, Charles Rogers, James Parrott, Felix Adler; directed by James W. Horne

☆

Lulubelle, it's you! I didn't recognize you standing up.

> **GROUCHO MARX** in *Go West* (1940): screenplay by
> Jack Jevne, Charles Rogers, James Parrott, Felix
> Adler; directed by Edward Buzzell

☆

I've seen women I'd look at quicker, but never one I'd look at longer.

> **CLARK GABLE** to Lana Turner in *Honky Tonk* (1941):
> screenplay by Marguerite Roberts and John
> Sanford; directed by Jack Conway

☆

Last night she was banging on my door for forty-five minutes—but I wouldn't let her out.

> **DEAN MARTIN** in *Kiss Me, Stupid* (1964): screenplay
> by Billy Wilder and I. A. L. Diamond; directed by
> Billy Wilder

☆

It's nights like this that drive men like me to women like you for nights like this.

> **BOB HOPE** to Hedy Lamarr in *My Favorite Spy*
> (1951): screenplay by Alan Jay Lerner,
> Edmund Hartmann, Jack Sher; directed by
> Norman Z. McLeod

☆

"I've never kissed a woman before."

"Before what?"

> **JOHN BEAL AND KATHARINE HEPBURN** in *The Little Minister* (1934): screenplay by Alan Jay Lerner, Jane Murfin, Sarah Y. Mason, Victor Heerman; directed by Richard Wallace

☆

"Did you say you can tear the telephone book in half?"

"Yessir."

"Wait a minute, wait a minute! You're tearing one page at a time."

"I ain't in a hurry."

> **EDDIE CANTOR AND HARRY EINSTEIN** (as Parkyakarkus) in *Strike Me Pink* (1936): screenplay by Alan Jay Lerner, Walter DeLeon, Francis Martin, Frank Butler; directed by Norman Taurog

☆

"I've changed my mind."

"Does it work any better?"

> **EDWARD ARNOLD AND MAE WEST** in *I'm No Angel* (1933): screenplay by Alan Jay Lerner, Mae West; directed by Wesley Ruggles

☆

Brave men run in my family.

> **BOB HOPE** in *The Paleface* (1948): screenplay by Edmund Hartmann, Frank Tashlin; directed by Norman Z. McLeod

☆

If I ever forgot myself with that girl, I'd remember it.

> **FRED ASTAIRE** about Ginger Rogers in *Top Hat*
> (1935): screenplay by Dwight Taylor and
> Allan Scott; directed by Mark Sandrich

☆

"Aren't you here early?"

"Oh, yes. Mr. Oxley's been complaining about my punctuation, so I'm careful to get here before nine."

> **CARY GRANT AND MARILYN MONROE** in
> *Monkey Business* (1952): screenplay by
> Ben Hecht, Charles Lederer, I. A. L.
> Diamond; directed by Howard Hawks

☆

"Is everybody in this world corrupt?"

"I don't know everybody."

> **HORST BUCHHOLZ** and Leon Askin in *One, Two,*
> *Three* (1961): screenplay by Billy Wilder and
> I. A. L. Diamond; directed by Billy Wilder

☆

"Most girls would give their eyes for a chance to see Monte."

"Wouldn't that rather defeat the purpose?"

> **FLORENCE BATES** and Lawrence Olivier in *Rebecca*
> (1940): screenplay by Joan Harrison and Robert
> Sherwood; directed by Alfred Hitchcock

☆

An associate producer is the only guy in Hollywood who will associate with the producer.

FRED ALLEN in *Sally, Irene and Mary* (1938): screenplay by Harry Tugend and Jack Yellen; directed by William A. Seiter

☆

I've married a few people I shouldn't have, but haven't we all? **MAMIE VAN DOREN,** actress

☆

Any actor who doesn't dare to make an enemy should get out of the business. **BETTE DAVIS,** actress

☆

I'm so damned sick of Katharine Hepburn, I'd like to kill her. On second thought, people have been so nice to me lately because they think I'm going to die. I think I'll stick around awhile and make the most of it.

KATHARINE HEPBURN, actress

☆

One thing's for sure—I hate talking about myself.

BARBRA STREISAND, singer, actress

☆

It's only the best fruit the birds pick at.

BETTE DAVIS, actress responding to criticism

☆

I never liked him and I always will,

> **DAVE CLARK,** actor, songwriter, performer
> with *The Dave Clark Five*

☆

"Did anyone ever tell you you dance like Ginger Rogers?"
"No, why?"
"No wonder."   **OLE OLSEN** and Martha Raye in *Hellzapoppin*
> (1941): screenplay by Nat Perrin and War-
> ren Wilson; directed by H. C. Potter

☆

Do you suppose I could buy back my introduction to
you?   **GROUCHO MARX** to Chico Marx in *Horsefeathers*
> (1932): screenplay by Bert Kalmar, Harry Ruby,
> S. J. Perelman, Will B. Johnstone; directed by
> Norman Z. McLeod

☆

SHE: "I've never been so insulted in all my life."
HE: "Well, it's early yet."

> **ESTHER MUIR** and Groucho Marx in *A Day at
> the Races* (1937): screenplay by Robert Pirosh,
> George Seaton, George Oppenheimer;
> directed by Sam Wood

☆

The actor Raymond Massey's face and frame were so close to the public idea of Lincoln, that when he portrayed *Abe Lincoln in Illinois* (1940), audiences grew to assume that Massey *was* Lincoln. Herman Mankiewicz, the wit, writer, and producer, was finally fed up and snapped: "Massey won't be satisfied until he's assassinated."

☆

Are you eating a tomato or is that your nose?

> **CHARLIE MCCARTHY** to W. C. Fields in *You Can't Cheat an Honest Man* (1939): screenplay by Everett Freeman, Richard Mack, George Marion Jr., and W. C. Fields; directed by George Marshall

☆

There are two good reasons why people go to see her. Those are enough.

> **HOWARD HUGHES,** producer, about bosomy star Jane Ruseell

☆

You're one of the most beautiful women I've ever seen, and that's not saying much for you.

> **GROUCHO MARX** to Margaret Dumont in *Animal Crackers* (1930): screenplay by Morrie Ryskind; directed by Victor Heerman

☆

If a gnat dived into your pool of knowledge, it would break its neck.

> **CARY GRANT** to Ginger Rogers in *Once Upon a Honeymoon* (1942): screenplay by Sheridan Gibney; directed by Leo McCarey

☆

I wanna be just like you. I figure all I need's a lobotomy and some tights.

> **JUDD NELSON** to high school wrestler Emilio Estevez in *The Breakfast Club*: screenplay by John Hughes; directed by John Hughes

☆

My Great Aunt Jennifer ate a whole box of candy every day of her life. She lived to be 102, and when she had been dead three days, she looked better than you do now.

> **MONTY WOOLLEY** to Mary Wickes in *The Man Who Came to Dinner* (1941): screenplay by Julius J. Epstein and Philip G. Epstein; directed by William Keighley

☆

Hell, I ain't paid to make good lines good. I'm paid to make bad lines sound good.

> **WALTER HUSTON,** Oscar-winning actor, father of director John Huston, grandfather of Angelica Huston

☆

On the screen he's perfect, yet on the set you'd swear that it's the worst job of acting in the history of motion pictures.

SAM WOOD, who directed Gary Cooper
in *The Pride of the Yankees* (1942)

☆

At my age [*he was in his nineties*] when I order a three-minute egg, they make me pay in advance.

GEORGE BURNS, actor, to Gene Shalit during
a *Today Show* interview NBC-TV

☆

Men aren't attracted to me for my mind, but for what I don't mind. **GYPSY ROSE LEE,** intellectual ecdysiast

☆

She's one of the nicest women I'm sorry I ever met.

HERMAN MANKIEWICZ, producer and writer,
about another producer's wife

☆

Don't miss it if you can. **DAVE CLARK,** actor, songwriter
of *The Dave Clark Five*

☆

It should have a big exciting finish—like an earthquake. A catechism of nature!

HARRY RAPF, MGM executive, advising
Herman Mankiewitz about a script

☆

At the Hollywood banquet celebrating his one-hundredth birthday, Adolph Zucker, one of the founding fathers of the motion picture business, said, "If I had known I was going to live this long, I would have taken better care of myself."

☆

A celebrity is a person who works hard all his life to become well known, then wears dark glasses to avoid being recognized.

FRED ALLEN comedian

☆

Film music should have the same relationship to the film drama that somebody's piano playing in my living room has on the book I am reading. **IGOR STRAVINSKY,** composer

☆

I can't listen to too much Wagner, ya know? I start to get the urge to conquer Poland.

WOODY ALLEN in *Manhattan Murder Mystery* (1998): screenplay and directed by Woody Allen

☆

I hate music, especially when it's played.

JIMMY DURANTE, comedian, "singer," actor

☆

Isn't it monstrous the way people go about saying things behind people's backs that are absolutely and entirely true.

> **GEORGE SANDERS** in *The Picture of Dorian Gray* (1945): written and directed by Albert Lewin

☆

I *am* big. It's the *pictures* that got small.

> **GLORIA SWANSON** as a faded movie queen in *Sunset Boulevard* (1950): screenplay by Charles Brackett, D. M. Marshman Jr., Billy Wilder; directed by Billy Wilder

Terms of Endearment

Although Hollywood is famous for its backbiting, it is also the scene of excessive backslapping. (At the Academy Awards ceremonies, stars have even mastered the chiropractic art of patting their own back.) No matter what the motion picture people may think of each other in private, they are lavish with praise for one another in public, their indiscriminate kisses of greeting making hand shaking passé. The following compliments sound genuine to the layman, but one never knows.

☆

For her [Greta Garbo], and her alone, I could have been a lesbian. **JOAN CRAWFORD,** actress

☆

The most beautiful female star in filmdom is Lassie. She transcends all boundaries; she's a totally sincere actress and at once a bitch and man's best friend. With gorgeous hair, yet."

PATSY KELLY, actress

☆

Walter [Matthau] can play *Richard III, Fiddler on the Roof, Charley's Aunt,* and *The Elephant Man* all in one afternoon. And in between he can squeeze in a few poker games.

BILLY WILDER, director

☆

Acting probably didn't come naturally to her, but the note of unsureness in what she did seemed to give her a certain childish attractiveness.　　　　**KING VIDOR,** director

on Hedy Lamar

☆

It took a little while to realize that he had perfected an elaborate camouflage to cover up one of the kindest and most generous of hearts.　　　　**DAVID NIVEN,** actor,

on Humphrey Bogart, actor

☆

I think Elizabeth is the only woman who ever costarred with my brother Warren Beatty who didn't go to bed with him. **SHIRLEY MacLAINE,** from the stage of New York's Palace Theater, after noting that Elizabeth Taylor, the actress, was in the audience

☆

What do dancers think of Fred Astaire? It's no secret. We hate him. He gives us a complex because he's too perfect. His perfection is an absurdity. It's too hard to face.

MIKHAIL BARYSHNIKOV, Russian ballet star, praising Fred Astaire, actor, dancer

☆

It's a great help for a man to be in love with himself. For an actor, it's absolutely essential.

ROBERT MORLEY deflecting remarks about his double chins

☆

It is true that Doris can come on strong, but like most people who come on strong, what she's really saying is, "Help me." And if you help her, everything's just fine.

ROCK HUDSON, actor, on Doris Day, actress

☆

In spite of having the usual womanly defects, she is the only really spiritually honest woman I have ever known.

VITTORIO DE SICA, director, praising
Sophia Loren, actress

☆

AUDREY HEPBURN: "Do you know what's wrong with you?"
CARY GRANT: "No. What?"
AUDREY HEPBURN: "Nothing."

Charade (1963): screenplay by Peter Stone;
directed by Stanley Donen

☆

Tallulah never bored anyone, and I consider that humanitarianism of a very high order indeed.

ANITA LOOS, eulogy for Tallulah Bankhead, actress

☆

A great lady. It's quite an achievement to spend that long in Hollywood and not become a Hollywood product. She always maneuvered around that—and that takes intelligence. She was always her own person.

DAVID NIVEN, actor,
on Audrey Hepburn, actress

☆

Mary Martin? Oh, she's all right . . . if you like talent.

her friend **ETHEL MERMAN,** actress

☆

Miss Merman is a great broad . . . that is, she's a great Broadway star.   her friend **MARY MARTIN**, actress

☆

Having been fascinated by the Alan Ladd phenomenon, I now had the opportunity to study it at close quarters. It turned out that he had the exquisite coordination and rhythm of an athlete, which made it a pleasure to watch him when he was being at all physical.

JAMES MASON on Alan Ladd, when they
costarred in *Botany Bay* (1953)

☆

For Bette Davis I wear my diamonds.

ANNA MAGNANI, actress,
on Bette Davis, actress

Woody Allen

(The Nonpareil)

By the second year of the third millennium A.D., Woody Allen had produced so large a number and variety of remarkable productions that he was destined to be enshrined in the *Great Writers and Directors Wing* of the Motion Picture Pantheon.

As 2002 ended, he had made thirty-two movies in thirty-three years. A "Best Picture" Oscar (*Annie Hall,* 1977), a "Best director" Oscar (*Annie Hall,* 1977), two Oscars for "Best Original Screenplay" (*Annie Hall,* 1977, and *Hannah and her Sisters,* 1986), and nineteen Oscar nominations for director or writer. Actors in casts under his direction had won five Oscars and fifteen acting nominations. Adding in all other categories as well, Woody Allen's pictures had won nine Academy Awards and forty-four Academy Award nominations. No other writer-director has come within miles of that achievement.

Unequaled are his series of films of life in New York City, in which the city itself is a central character. And no writer has created so disparate a range of characters, from touching to touched. The supernal quality of his humor and wit in screenplays, short stories, and essays are, well, supernal—(how many chances does one have to use that word?). Go get 'em, Woody.

☆

It is impossible to experience one's own death objectively and still carry a tune. **WOODY ALLEN,** from *My Philosophy*

☆

Years ago, my mother gave me a bullet. I put it in my breast pocket. Two years after that, I was walking down the street when a berserk evangelist heaved a Gideon Bible out a hotel room window, hitting me in the chest. The Bible would've gone through my heart if it wasn't for the bullet.

WOODY ALLEN, Monologue

☆

I'm what you call a teleological existential atheist. I believe that there's an intelligence to the universe with the exception of certain parts of New Jersey.

WOODY ALLEN in *Sleeper* (1973): written by Woody Allen, Marshall Brickman; directed by Woody Allen

☆

If only God would give me some clear sign! Like making a large deposit in my name at a Swiss bank.

WOODY ALLEN

☆

I've had sixteen fights and I won all of them but twelve.

> **MICHAEL RAPAPORT** *Mighty Aphrodite* (1995):
> screenplay by Woody Allen; directed by
> Woody Allen

☆

WOODY ALLEN: "I got a job at a striptease. I help the girls dress and undress."

PETER O'TOOLE: "Nice job."

WOODY ALLEN: "Twenty francs a week."

PETER O'TOOLE: "Not very much."

WOODY ALLEN: "It's all I can afford."

> In *What's New, Pussycat?* (1965): screenplay by
> Woody Allen; directed by Clive Donner

☆

I'm gonna give him one more year and then I'm going to Lourdes.
WOODY ALLEN, in *Annie Hall*, on his
psychoanalyst of many years

☆

The lion and the calf shall lie down together, but the calf won't get much sleep.
WOODY ALLEN

☆

More than any other time in history, mankind faces a crossroads. One path leads to despair and utter hopelessness. The other, to total extinction. Let us pray we have the wisdom to choose correctly. **WOODY ALLEN**

☆

HIGH MACHER: Good afternoon. I'm the Grand Exalted High Macher of Raspar, a non-existent but real-sounding country. Yes. We're on a waiting list. As soon as there's an opening on the map, we're next. It's rough on a new country. Do you realize the entire population is still packed in crates?

PHIL MOSCOWITZ: Good luck. I'm sure you'll get your country on the globe.

HIGH MACHER: Thank You. I'm hoping for something between Spain and Greece. It's really much warmer there. **WOODY ALLEN**'s *What's Up, Tiger Lily?* (1966)

☆

VOICEOVER: "Chapter One: He adored New York City. He idolized it all out of proportion." Uh, no, make that: "He romanticized it all out of proportion. Now, to him, no matter what the season was, this was still a town that existed in black and white and pulsated to the great tunes of George Gershwin." Ah, now let me start this over.

"Chapter One: He was too romantic about Manhattan as he was about everything else. He thrived on the hustle-bustle of the crowds and the traffic.

"To him, New York meant beautiful women and street-smart guys who seemed to know all the angles." Nah, no . . . corny, too corny for my taste. I mean, let me try to be more profound. . . .

"Chapter One: He was as tough and romantic as the city he loved. Behind his black-rimmed glasses was the coiled sexual power of a jungle cat." I love this. "New York was his town. And it always would be."

> **WOODY ALLEN,** opening narration in *Manhattan*
> (1979), written and directed by Woody Allen

☆

Someone once asked me if my dream was to live on in the hearts of my people, and I said I would like to live on in my apartment. And that's really what I would prefer.

> **ROLLING STONE** interview

☆

NOTE: Also see Woody Allen under "The Sweet Bye and Bye," starting on page 87, and "S*X" on page 103 et seq.

"I Do Wish You Would Decline Alcohol."
"Okay. Drink, Drank, Drunk."

Hollywood is on the wagon. For decades, alcohol was a mixture of comedy (any W. C. Fields movie), a warning (*The Lost Weekend*), or a badge of sophistication (*The Thin Man* series). It's diminished in recent years. Lots of beer on screen now (with brand labels showing). But very litle liquor.

In the dear old days, whatever the occasion, on screen or off, Fields got into high spirits (and vice versa). He reported that he had lost his corkscrew during a long trip, and lamented, "We lived for days on nothing but food and water."

☆

As *The Bank Dick* (1940), Fields waddled into his favorite saloon and asked,

"Was I in here last night, and did I spend a twenty dollar bill?"

"Yeah."

"Oh boy, what a load that is off my mind. I thought I'd lost it." Screenplay by Mahatma Kane Jeeves (W. C. Fields), directed by Edward Cline

☆

Well, he didn't get that nose from playing ping-pong.

SUSAN MILLER asking Margaret Dumont if W. C. Fields drinks in *Never Give a Sucker an Even Break* (1941): screenplay by Prescott Chaplin; story by Otis Criblecoblis (W. C. Fields); directed by Edward Cline

☆

In *International House* (1933), Peggy Hopkins Joyce invites Fields to join her in a glass of wine. "You get in first," Fields says, "and if there's room enough, I'll join you."

Screenplay by Neil Brant, Louis Jeifetz, Walter Deleon, Francis Martin; directed by Edward Sutherland

☆

Let's get something to eat. I'm thirsty.

WILLIAM POWELL in *After the Thin Man* (1936): screenplay by Frances Goodrich and Albert Hackett; directed by W. S. Van Dyke

☆

MYRNA LOY: "I got rid of all those reporters."
WILLIAM POWELL: "What did you tell them?"
MYRNA LOY: "We're out of scotch."

> *Another Thin Man* (1939): screenplay by
> Frances Goodrich and Albert Hackett;
> directed by W. S. Van Dyke

☆

OLIVER HARDY: "You drank it all! We were supposed to share it."
STAN LAUREL: "I couldn't help it. My half was on the bottom."   *Men O'War* (1929): screenplay by Leo McCarey and H. M. Walker; directed by Lewis R. Foster

☆

I've been drinking over forty years, and I haven't acquired the habit yet.

> **GUY KIBBEE** in *Joy of Living* (1938): screenplay by
> C. Graham Baker, Allan Scott, Gene Towne;
> directed by Tay Garnett

☆

The cost of living has gone up another dollar a quart.

> **W. C. FIELDS,** unique comic actor, writer, juggler

☆

"Whiskey is slow poison."

"So who's in a hurry?"

> **FRED ALLEN AND ROBERT BENCHLEY** in *It's in the Bag*
> (1945): screenplay by Jay Dratler, Alma Reville,
> Morrie Ryskind; directed by Richard Wallace

☆

I've had hangovers before, but this time even my hair
hurts.

> **ROCK HUSDSON** in *Pillow Talk* (1959): screenplay
> by Clarence Greene, Maurice Richlin,
> Russell Rouse, Stanley Shapiro; directed by
> Michael Gordon

☆

"Could you be persuaded to have a drink, dear?"

"Well, maybe just a tiny triple."

> **LUCILLE BALL** in *Mame* (1974): screenplay by
> Paul Zindel; directed by Gene Saks

☆

ACTOR: "What would your father have said if he knew that
you drank two quarts of whiskey a day?"

W. C. FIELDS: "He would have said I was a sissy."

☆

BARTENDER, SERVING FIELDS A DRINK: "Would you like
a piece of lemon peel in it?"

FIELDS: "If I wanted lemonade, I'd ask for it."

☆

I know I've had enough when my knees bend backward.

W. C FIELDS, unique comic actor, writer, juggler

☆

Wouldn't it be terrible if I quoted some reliable statistics which prove that more people are driven insane through religious hysteria than by drinking alcohol?

W. C. FIELDS, unique comic actor, writer, juggler

☆

Everybody should believe in something; I believe I'll have another drink.   **ROBERT BENCHLEY,** humorist, actor, author

☆

I drink too much. Will you tell me one great actor who doesn't drink?   **ROBERT SHAW,** actor

☆

I'm no alcoholic, I'm a drunkard. The difference is, drunkards don't go to meetings.

JACKIE GLEASON, actor, comedian

☆

If four or five guys tell you that you're drunk, even though you know you haven't had a thing to drink, the least you can do is to lie down a little while.

JOSEPH SCHENCK, chief of 20th Century-Fox

We Need One (at least) New Oscar Category

The Razor's Edge (1946) won four Oscar nominations. The film authority John Malone suggests the picture deserved a fifth award, in a new category called *Surviving a Line of Dialogue Almost Impossible to Say with a Straight Face*. Tyrone Power would have won a nomination for making it through, "The dead look so terribly dead when they're dead."

Other Nominees in This Category

★ The hopeful Israelite ready to flee Egypt in *The Ten Commandments* (1956): "We're going to the land of milk and honey. Anybody know the way?"

★ George Kennedy in *Earthquake* (1974): "Earthquakes bring out the worst in some guys."

★ Lloyd Nolan to Lana Turner in *Peyton Place* (1968): "Everybody reacts differently to suicide. With Allison, it's severe shock."

★ Tony Perkins to Tuesday Weld in *Pretty Poison* (1968): "If I didn't really work for the government, if I was just a guy who accidentally killed his parents, would you still love me?"

★ Demi Moore in *Striptease* (1996) complains about her ex-husband who's out with her daughter: "Then he drives around with her in that van of his, drinking, taking pills—I'm sure he doesn't think about putting a seat belt on her."

★ Rex Harrison (as Pope Julius II) to Charlton Heston (as Michelangelo) in *The Agony and the Ecstasy* (1965): screenplay by Philip Dunne, directed by Carol Reed. "You dare to dicker with your Pontiff?"

★ Question to Charlton Heston in *The Agony and the Ecstasy* (1965): "Michelangelo, make up your mind, once and for all, do you want to finish that ceiling?"

★ Victor Mature to Hedy Lamarr in *Samson and Delilah* (1949): "Delilah, what a dimpled dragon you can be, flashing fire and smoke."

★ Anne Baxter to Charlton Heston in *The Ten Commandments* (1956): "Oh, Moses, Moses, you stubborn, splendid, adorable fool."

Bibliography

For decades I've made notes from books, magazines, newspapers. I've reviewed films into the thousands. After years of reading and hearing so much—from obits to Ovitz—I grew unable to differentiate *copyright* from *copycat*. I have done my honest best, and I made this list of sources as complete as my memory allows. I wish I had been born with more RAM. If I have been guilty of any improper usage, it has been innocent guilt, and I hereby apologize and offer restitution, either by endlessly writing the offending quotation on the blackboard, or by serving time. I take refuge in the views of my learned predecessors:

☆

When a thing has been said and well said, have no scruple; take it and copy it. Give references? Why should you?

Either your readers know where you have taken the passage and the precaution is needless, or they do not know and you humiliate them.　**ANATOLE FRANCE** (1844–1924)

Plagiarists, at least, have the merit of preservation.

BENJAMIN DISRAELI (1804–81)

Fine Words! I wonder where you stole them.

JONATHAN SWIFT (1667–1745)

Goethe said there would be little of him if he were to discard what he owed to others.　**CHARLOTTE CUSHMAN**

Professor Brander Matthews was discussing plagiarism with Nicholas Murray Butler.* "In the case of the first man to use an anecdote there is originality; in the case of the second, there is plagiarism; with the third, it is lack of originality; and with the fourth, it is drawing from a common stock."

"Yes," interjected Butler, "and in the case of the fifth, it is research."

---

*President of Columbia University from 1902 to 1945, advisor to seven presidents, decorated by fifteen foreign governments, honorary degrees from thirty-seven colleges and universities, member of more than fifty learned societies, and winner of the Nobel Peace Prize. Nothing to do with this book, but I find his life and accomplishments irresistible.

Adamson, Joe. *Groucho, Harpo, Chico, and Sometimes Zeppo.* New York: Simon & Schuster, 1973.

Anobile, Richard J. *A Flask of Fields.* N.p.: Darian, House, 1972.

Bainbridge, Jim. *Show Me the Money: A Century of Great Movie Lines.* N.p.: Woodford Press, 1999.

Berlin, Joey. *Toxic Fame.* Detroit: Visible Ink Press, 1996.

Berg, Scott. *Goldwyn: A Biography.* N.p.: Knopf, 1989.

Boller, P. F. and R. L. Davis. *Hollywood Anecdotes.* N.p.: 1988.

Byrne, Robert. *The 2,548 Best Things Anybody Ever Said.* New York: Galahad Books, 1996.

Carroll, Brenden G. *The Last Prodigy.* Portland, Oregon: Amadeus Press, 1997.

Cassell Dictionary of Human Quotations, Nigel Rees, ed. N.p. Continuum International Publishing Group, 1999.

Cerf, Bennett. *Bennett Cerf's The Life of the Party.* N.p.: Doubleday, 1956.

Cerf, Bennett. *The Laugh's On Me.* New York: Doubleday, 1959.

Charlton, James, ed. *The Writer's Quotation Book.* New York: Pushcart Press, 1980.

Chieger, Bob. *Was It Good for You?* New York: Atheneum Books, 1983.

Colombo, John Robert. *Popcorn in Paradise.* [N.p.: Holt Rinehart Winston, 1980].

Corey, Melinda, and George Ochoa. *The Dictionary of Film Quotations.* New York: Three Rivers Press, 1995.

Davis Jr., Sammy. *Yes I Can.* N.p.: Farrar Straus & Giroux, 1965.

Drennan, Robert E. *The Algonquin Wits.* New York: Citadel, 1968.

Edwards, K. *I Wish I'd Said That.* N.p.: Abelard, 1976.

Eells, George, and S. Musgrove. *Mae West.* N.p.: 1989.

An Encyclopedia of Quotations About Music. Nat Shapiro, ed. New York: Doubleday & Company, 1978.

Familiar Quotations. Edited by John Bartlett. N.p.: Little, Brown, 1980.

Freedland, Michael. *The Goldwyn Touch: A Biography of Sam Goldwyn.* N.p.: Harrap, 1986.

Goldstein, Malcolm. *George S. Kaufman.* New York: Oxford University Press, 1979.

Goodman, Ezra. *The Fifty-Year Decline and Fall of Hollywood.* New York: Simon & Schuster, 1961.

Graham, Shiela. *The Rest of the Story.* New York: Coward McCann, 1964.

Green, Marc. *Hollywood Dynasties.* N.p.: Delilah Books, 1984.

Hadleigh, Boze. *Hollywood Babble On.* New York: Berkley Publishing Group, 1994.

Hample, Stuart. *All the Sincerity in Hollywood . . .* Colorado: Fulcrum Publishing, 2001.

Hay, Peter. *Theatrical Anecdotes.* New York: Oxford University Press, 1987.

Herman, Gary. *The Book of Hollywood Quotes: The Insults, the Insights, the Famous Lines.* N.p.: Omnibus Press, 1979.

Herrmann, Dorothy *S. J. Perelman: A Life.* New York; Simon & Schuster, 1986.

Herrmann, Dorothy. *With Malice Toward All.* New York: G. P. Putnam's Sons: 1982.

Jarski, Rosemarie. *Wisecracks.* Licolnwood, Ill.: Contempory Books, 1999.

Johnston, Alva. *The Great Goldwyn.* New York: Arno Press, 1978.

Levant, Oscar. *The Memoirs of an Amnesiac.* New York: G. P. Putnam's Sons, 1965.

Levant, Oscar. *The Unimportance of Being Oscar.* New York: G. P. Putnam's Sons, 1968.

Manchester, William. *The Last Lion.* Boston: Little, Brown, 1983.

Marsh, Clive, and Gaye Ortiz, eds. *Explorations in Theology and Film: Movies and Meaning.* N.p.: Blackwell Publishers, 1997.

Marx, Groucho. *Groucho and Me.* New York: Simon & Schuster, 1989.

McClelland, Doug. *Star Speak: Hollywood on Everything.* Boston and London: Faber and Faber, 1987.

Meredith, Scott. *George S. Kaufman and the Algonquin Round Table.* New York: Doubleday, 1974.

Meryman, Richard. *Mank.* New York: William Morrow, 1978.

Molly, Haskell, and Ed Sikov. *Screwball: Hollywood's Madcap Romantic Comedies.* New York: Crown Publishers, 1989.

The Oxford Dictionary of Humorous Quotations. Edited by Ned Sherrin. N.p.: Oxford University Press, 2001.

Penguin Dictionary of Modern Humorous Quotations. Fred Metcalf, ed. 1987.

Peter, Dr. Laurence J. *Peter's Quotations; Ideas for our Time.* N.p.: William Morrow, 1977.

Petras, Kathryn, and Ross Petras. *The 776 Stupidest Things Ever Said.* N.p.: Main Street Books, Doubleday. 1993.

Petras, Kathryn, and Ross Petras. *The 776 Even Stupider Things Ever Said.* N.p.: HarperCollins, 1994.

Petras, Kathryn, and Ross Petras. *The 776 Nastiest Things Ever Said.* N.p.: HarperCollins, 1995.

Petras, Kathryn, and Ross Petras. *Stupid Celebrities: Over 500 of the Most Idiotic Things Ever Said by Famous People.* N.p.: Andrews McMeel Publishing, 1998.

Petras, Kathryn, and Ross Petras. *Stupid Movie Lines.* New York: Villard, 1999.

Rosten, Leo. *Rome Wasn't Burned in a Day; The Mischief of Language.* N.p.: Doubleday, 1972.

Rosten, Leo. *Leo Rosten's Carnival of Wit.* N.p.: Penguin Books USA, 1994.

Roth, K. Madsen, ed. *Hollywood Wits.* New York: Avon Books, 1995.

Schwartz, Carol, and Jim Olenski, eds. *Video Hound's Cult Flicks and Trash Pics*, N.p.: Visible Ink Press, 2002.

Shapiro, Nat, ed. *Whatever It Is, I'm against It.* N.p.: Simon & Schuster, 1984.

Sherrin, Ned. *Cutting Edge.* N.p. J. M. Dent and Sons, 1984.

Shipman, David. *Movie Talk.* St. Martin's Press, 1988.

Simon, Neil. *The Collected Plays of Neil Simon.* New York: Penguin Group, 1979.

Simpson, James B. *Simpson's Contemporary Quotations: The Most Notable Quotes Since 1950.* N.p.: Houghton Mifflin, 1988.

Stapleton, Maureen, and Jane Scovell. *A Hell of a Life.* New York: Simon & Schuster, 1995.

Stephens, Autumn. *Drama Queens.* California: Conari Press, 1998.

Stephens, Autumn. *Loose Cannons.* New York: MJF Books, 1998.

Sullivan, George. *Quotable Hollywood.* New York: Barnes & Noble, 2001.

Sunshine, Linda, ed. *The Illustrated Woody Allen Reader.* New York: Alfred A. Knopf, 1993.

Teichmann, Howard. *George S. Kaufman.* N.p.: McClelland and Stewart, 1972.

Thomas, Bob. *King Cohn.* New York: G. P. Putnam's Sons, 1967.

Thomas, Bob. *Thalberg; Life and Legend.* N.p.: Doubleday 1969.

Thomson, David. *A Biographical Dictionary of Film.* New York: Alfred A. Knopf, 1994.

Wiley, Mason, and Damien Bona. *Inside Oscar.* New York: Ballantine, 1998.

Wilk, Max. *The Wit and Wisdom of Hollywood.* N.p.: Kingsport Press, 1971.

Winokur, Jon. *The Portable Curmudgeon.* New York: Penguin Group, 1987.

Winokur, Jon. *True Confessions.* New York: Penguin Group, 1992.

Zierold, Norman. *The Hollywood Tycoons.* London: Hamilton, 1969.

Zolotow, Maurice. *Billy Wilder in Hollywood.* N.p.: Putnam, 1977.

Can't Do It Alone

The witty, sharp-tongued, malapropped, wise-cracking, stumble-speaking men and women of the movies have (in the words of Yogi Berra) made this book necessary. Above all, a tilt of the beret to the many accomplished women and men who have written screenplays over the last eighty-five years of the twentieth century and thereby put memorable dialogue into the mouths of actresses and actors, many of whom still believe they thought of the words themselves.

There can be no good movie without a good script, and there is no good script without a good writer. The public praises the actress in a comedy ("My, isn't she clever!"), while the writer works in anonymity. But it's the writer who is so "My, isn't she clever." I am proud that every movie line in this book is followed by the name(s) of the writer(s). Let credit be stowed where it belongs.

I salute Bill Adler of Bill Adler Books, a clever man with a company name, who had the nerve to write to me with the idea. It was he who negotiated the pittance that we will receive for such copies as may not end up in the Strand, Fred Bass's famous repository of previously read books and remainders, at 828 Broadway in New York City.

I lift my lid to John Malone of the great state of Pennsylvania for his assiduousness in digging up so many funny remarks, for his sense of humor, and for being a pleasure to correspond with.

I embrace my long-time pal, Howard Greene, for his meticulous proofreading. I thank him for his many good suggestions—additions and deletions—and for his psychological support. Anyone who sets out to assemble this sort of anthology needs all the psychological help he can get.

I thank my friends at the libraries in Lenox, Massachusetts, and Pittsfield, Massachusetts, who helped me to track down so many sources, and whom I have repaid by erasing all of my pencil marks in their books and periodicals.

Many bows to my Massachusetts assistant Jennifer Slonski: diligent, unflappable under pressure, unerringly organized, cheerful and always on target—indispensable.

Deep appreciation to my good friend and New York assistant, Samantha Holman, who plays the archives the way Sir James Galway plays the flute. She uncovered quotes forgotten even by the people who had said them. And is Sam fast.

A hearty handshake and an admiring clasp on the shoulder for Steve Snider, vice president and creative director of

St. Martin's Press, for the snazzy cover, for his art direction throughout, and for pointing out the many duplications that I had put in before I discovered that I was not being paid by the word.

Nichole Argyres of St. Martin's Press kept me on schedule (give or take six months) with her equanimity and diplomatic prodding. Nichole: my gratitude and many snappy salutes.

I come to praise Diane Higgins, my ace editor at St. Martin's Press, whom I haven't seen lately but assume she is the one with the bald head, having yanked out her hair as I missed deadline after deadline after deadline. Patience, thy name is Diane.

The End